Trump Over Biden

The Logical Comparison

10 Reasons for Trump
10 Strikes Against Biden

Dedicated to Thomas the Eternal Paine

Table of Contents

Introduction

Freedom and opportunity are the pinnacles of governance wherever they lead we should follow. On the contrary, partisan politics leads us to the pitfalls of humanity. People become rigid when flexibility is required. Unseen facts appear at random, and ideas must adapt in the face of incontrovertible evidence. After years of thoughtful research, I seek truth as an American, not a partisan.

Being a conservative is like training at the gym. It requires a painful input (x) but offers a rewarding output (y). Let us take an issue, for example, building up the military. The input (x) requires painstaking research, funding, and training. But the output (y) is peace. The world's strongest military is a badge of honor few countries have ever adorned. It offers us world peace and prosperity through strength.

Liberals are the opposite. They get all their gratification from the input (x) and endure the output (y). For instance, the abhorrent idea of abolishing the police, the input (x) of liberating people, from what they falsely perceive to be an overbearing racist police department makes them feel like heroes. They proudly chant their slogans with emotional conviction after having defeated a figment of their imagination. However, the output (y) of living in a community without police is horrible. Criminals feed off this weakness and things quickly devolve into mayhem.

This is a theme throughout the left / right political divide. Whether it be welfare, justice reform, or walls. Liberals are great at tearing things down, and conservatives are great at building things up. Sometimes it is a bad build like a system that does not allow women the right to vote. Both sides have their usefulness.

Today's liberals are focused on tearing down the police force, but instead of destroying it, we should build it up because we cannot live a civilized life without it. People need to accept that our police force will never be perfect because it is composed of humans and we are inherently imperfect. The only solution to perfection would be a robot police force that is programmed to act judiciously. Until then, we must force these out of control clusters to calm down and be reasonable.

The people that surround us in our families and communities have subconscious control over our political decisions. They can trick us into believing the most illogical things. It is this fabric where the partisan mind lives. People spread lies so fast they solidify and become false truths. The actual truth foils this plan, therefore partisans condemn it as hate speech.

When a fact exists, that destroys my point of view: I must either contend with that fact, find someone who can or surrender my point of view. There is no room for anger or spite of things presented as facts. Living in a toxic bubble that bends the truth and ignores key details of reality is counterproductive to our forward progression.

In this book, I will take a stand for Donald Trump. I leave it to my contemporaries to counter my viewpoint. Perhaps they can offer a reasonable alternative to which I will rebut. Thus, the conversation continues. I would never call for the silencing of any opposition, and we should universally shame anyone who does.

Debates are a necessary part of our political discourse, they allow us to explore each candidate. We must begin with an open mind so we can pay close attention to integrity, confidence, honesty, and direction. Integrity is important in any human interaction. Will you do what you say you are going to do? When the journey becomes difficult, will you quit? Have you flip-flopped? Why?

The facts I present here will have little effect on the far-left and far-right. Once a person becomes deeply partisan, they lose objectivity. They are convinced of an egregious guilt and seal their thoughts with anger. Many partisans have convinced themselves that Trump is an updated version of Hitler. To eliminate this mass hysteria would require months of counseling, a deprogramming of sorts. The partisan hacks know this and work tirelessly to reprogram people. Hijacking their minds to commit evil acts. It has already begun with senseless destruction of property, attacking people, and even murder.

While I support Trump it is not a blind allegiance; it is measured and practical because of his platform. As a mathematician, I will explain it this way: I focus on his results, the output (y). Think of both candidates as the input variables (x), the White House represents the function (f(x)), and what we gain from it all is the output (y). Many partisans will focus on Trump being an egregious x-variable, but the actual effect of having Trump as president (y) is a net positive.

I have invoked the mathematical function (f(x)) to give us a deeper understanding of my political philosophy. The function (f(x)) can be thought of as a machine which takes an input (x) and does something to it to produce and output (y). A simple diagram of this: (x) —> (f(x)) —> (y). The x-variable (x) goes into the machine (f(x)) and produces the output (y). Think about making a smoothie, it starts with some fruit (x) which is put into the blender (f(x)) and outcomes a smoothie (y).

The purpose of looking at the x-variable is to predict the y-variable. Other than that, the x is useless. People that hate Trump are always focusing on his x-value using it to divide us. They speak of how he is unpresidential, racist, or misogynistic, and therefore his output (y) as president should be racist and misogynistic. But it is not, and they hate him all the more for it. He insults their pride and makes them look like liars. They become angrier by the day because of his positive achievements. This leads to Trump derangement syndrome or a broken function which we can symbolize as the empty set Ø .

The elite establishment hates him because he goes against their interest. They will deny this because to admit it is to confess their interest, which counters our interest. The truth is Trump's output (y) aligns with most Americans, thus the media must ignore or distort it. They footnote all his victories with a negative twist. They can never just give him credit when he deserves it. Nancy Pelosi called his Middle East Peace deal a "distraction." He will probably not win the Nobel Peace Prize, despite Barack Obama winning one just for being elected.

His vision will lead to freedom and prosperity. If one could prove otherwise, then I would change course. Not being able to say the same proves partisanship. I would be a socialist if you could prove that socialism leads to a brighter future. However, it does not. It only works in a university laboratory.

Socialism comes from focusing on the input: helping the underprivileged (x), and ignoring the output: economic collapse (y). Ironically socialism creates more of the thing it was intended to stop: suffering. As it happens, turning an imperfect world upside-down to create perfect outcomes has dramatically negative consequences. Seems like we forget this from time to time.

The greatest truth of all is that we as a society must find a balance in our politics. Too much power by either the left or right and we lose freedom. Politics is like an amplifier's equalizer; we must fine-tune the settings; too far to one side and we go out of tune. After listening to both sides, I believe we need more conservatives to counter the radical partisan agenda on the left.

I write independently, free from outside restraints as I have no connections to any political circles. I do not care who I offend, my only mission is to find the truth. In, Trump v. Biden it is Trump by a landslide. I will prove this unequivocally.

1

The Art of Trump

Personal History

Donald John Trump was born in Queens, New York, and would go on to become our 45th president. He grew up in a competitive American family. His desire for success has been the driving narrative of his life, and winning creates bitter rivals and sore losers. Trump's wake is filled with them. They go on for hours with their emotional grievances and fact-less diatribes. His niece wrote an entire book proving she is a bitter person.

Judging from the success of his children, Trump appears to be a great father. He does not drink or do drugs. He is sober and engaged politically. Perhaps another reason liberals hate him. He is actively involved in countering their narratives. Listening to him speak, we get the sense that he is intelligent with a balanced IQ and EQ. He is not a demented person with a psychological disorder, as the "Goldwater Rule" violating armchair-psychologist would have us believe.

After taking over the family business in 1971, Trump would greatly expand it to achieve a personal wealth of $2 to $10 billion, depending on who you ask. The basic facts cannot even be agreed upon because he has made the left so irrational. We live in a time when cold hard facts cannot overcome illogical irate feelings. The media is obsessed with gotcha moments. Tallying his lie total to be 20,000 at last count.

Within those 20,000 lies, which one is the worst? And what was the consequence of it? Countless articles speak of lies, but there is no mention of an egregious one that caused harm. Trump uses hyperbolic predictions to make political points. He simplifies things so that the American people can easily understand it. Many of these things are not lies but more of political opinions.

In particular, Trump spoke of Joe Biden and Bernie Sanders wanting to abolish the police. Neither man has been on record for defunding the police. However, they both speak of changing and reforming the police.

In particular, Biden has flip-flop-flipped on this important issue. To begin, he wrote an op-ed in 2002 calling for more police. This did not sit well with his 2020 base so in an interview he agreed to "divert" funding from police. Divert is doublespeak for defund, and then his campaign put out a statement saying he does not support defunding the police. Which one is it? I know the Joe Biden of old is a law and order guy but his campaign knows this will not play well for his "anything but Trump" supporters.

Many of his supporters have outright called for dismantling the police and abolishing the prison system. A horrible idea that would create chaos. Biden and Sanders are both to weak to push back on the far-left over anything. In fact, Biden's choice of Kamala Harris provides further evidence for Trump's argument. She uses the phrase "reimaging policing," which centers around reducing the number of police and therefore is a defunding of the police. This term is a smokescreen that creates confusion. The far-left thinks they are getting defunding, and the center-right thinks they are getting reforms. Thus, a Biden/Harris ticket is a vote for defunding.

There is a simple truth here that supporting Biden is tantamount to defunding the police, not supporting it, or changing it so much that it will be abolished. Why? Because Biden will have limited control for a limited time over his administration. The people that surround him and support Democrats, in general, are intentionally antagonistic to the police and other federal agencies such as ICE. The people he would appoint to the justice department would systematically change it in such a way as to essentially abolish it. He would be helpless to stop it, and therefore Trump's point is valid while the letter of his words might not be completely accurate. To explain all the nuance behind it requires a book. In a short tweet, he can lump Harris/Biden with antagonizing, defunding, distorting, or abolishing police agencies, which is what will happen under their administration.

It is reasonable to assume that Democrats will cave-in to the political pressures of the left and destroy our justice system, which is unfeasible considering they do not have a cohesive message on how to replace it. Chanting "no justice no peace" does not spontaneously produce the perfect justice system. Some have called for using unarmed social workers in extraordinarily dangerous domestic disputes. After a few of these people get caught in the crossfire, there will be a call to arm them.

What is more, when traveling to dire events they would need to speed through intersections. Thus, we could equip their cars with lights to warn other drivers. We could make the lights blue and red so that they stand out. They would need uniforms so that civilians could distinguish them from suspects. They would also need to be able to detain people with handcuffs, and put them in the back of cars to take them to secure holding places. One of these suspects might violently resist detainment and be killed. Then we must take to the streets and burn everything to the ground. After starting all over again, what have we done but drive around in a circle to please an angry mob?

Alternatively, others have called for outright anarchy. They want to live in a movie like *The Purge.* Where people will be hunted like animals for their wealth. They have already tried this in Seattle with CHOP. It was a complete disaster. We need law and order to function as a civilized society. Mob rule is a very dangerous thing, the history books are full of their atrocities.

When criminals are shown kindness, they repay it by wreaking havoc on our city streets. Everyday Americans will be the victims of an uptick in violence. Millions of people that were unaware of the importance of politics. What are these politicians really saying? Trump eats away at the covert narrative running beneath the stream of the left. They are antagonistic to the systems of justice such as the police and prisons. They do not believe in punishing or spanking. They reject the saying, "spare the rod, spoil the child," and consequently, we have a plethora of undisciplined criminals running around.

They constantly speak of how America has the most prisoners in the world per capita, never speaking of the fact that many other countries simply execute people without countless appeals and years on death row. Our prison population is about 2.3 million in a country of 330 million. That is about 0.7%. This is not an astronomical number, especially when we consider that about 1-2% of almost any population will break the law for any number of reasons without fear of consequence. If you add the fear of consequence in a strict society, we can reduce that number, but we end up trampling freedoms. We must find a balance in this equation. One where we are not unduly punishing people but also not showing weakness to criminals. Removing the fear of consequence could increase the number of criminals. The remaining people have good character and would only break laws if social norms forced them to.

America's Advocate

On the world stage, Trump is a great advocate for America. He is an excellent deal-maker, understanding how to use flattery and leverage in negotiations. He plays the game of world politics by being positive and thinking big. However, he also anticipates worst-case scenarios and reserves the power to walk away from deals.

He understands the mathematical probability of things falling apart, so he keeps his options open. He does not like negotiating from a position of weakness, therefore, he uses leverage to gain the upper hand. He understands that the press loves a sensational story, so he is just bold enough to pique their interest. Living by the mantra, "bad press is better than no press." He is a counter-puncher and fights back when mistreated. He is frugal and gets a thrill from winning the game, not making the money. He also delivers on his promises.

He promised to withdraw from the Iran Nuclear Deal and he did. He also withdrew troops from the Middle East changing the tone. He declared the dawn of the new middle east by brokering a peace agreement between Israel and two Arab countries. The deal with the United Arab Emirates and Bahrain will include trade, security and tourism. Muslims will be allowed to visit Islamic holy sites in Jerusalem. This could be a lasting legacy for Trump. Finally peace in the Middle East.

Trump could accomplish many great things if the partisan hatred did not slow him down so much. All of his flaws are superficial, there is nothing in his personality that is harmful to us as a nation. The harm comes from a wildly out of control left-wing reaction. They prance around our city streets with their toddler-like temper tantrums targeting our institutions to tear down, angry because they bought into a "Dangerous Donald" narrative.

The Clinton Campaign started this narrative in 2016. The strategy was to paint the opponent too deplorable to vote for. The left then made huge leaps in logic to grow The Dangerous Deplorable Donald Narrative. It was pumped into media outlets and spread through our society like a virus. Random street parrots chant, "Trump is a racist." They have no facts or logic behind their accusations. What has Trump ever done that is racist? Then they chant, "Russia Russia Russia!" The world was supposed to end because of him, and yet here we are standing strong three quarters through one of the craziest years ever.

The left relies heavily on emotion. The Dangerous Donald and glass ceiling narrative combined to form a fountain of bitterness which we are still witnessing. The mob wants revenge even after three years. They refuse to give Trump a chance to improve our nation. If they could forget the x-variable and focus on his results, we could make great strides around the world.

Trump is not allowed to be successful because of the number of people that would have to "eat crow." There were so many apocalyptic predictions that mislead us. Trump producing results makes them look like fools. The newspapers portrayed him as a failed businessman with multiple bankruptcies. This is the beginning of a long and misleading narrative about Trump. How does generating a wealth of over 2 billion dollars equate to being a business failure? If that defines failure then what is success? Does it matter? Why are we supposed to care if his wealth is 2 billion or 4 billion? Only partisan hacks wade into these waters.

There are legitimate criticisms to be made about any human as we are all inherently imperfect, but it needs to be legitimate, and not obsessive emotional insanity known as Trump Derangement Syndrome. Feelings are not facts. The left lives in these interconnected webs of propaganda, and if anyone dares question them, they shut down or become emotional and lash out. They want everyone to live in their fact-free bubble. That is why they are antagonistic to the first amendment. Politics has turned into religion for them.

Trump's personal life does not affect him as a leader, or me as a citizen, therefore I will not entertain them. How many wives he has had or women he has slept with or locker room banter he has engaged in makes him human. It does not make him some unclean deplorable incapable of leadership. This idea of a clean, perfect human leading us is a fool's mirage.

Building things can be a messy endeavor. Even our great forefathers who built the most incredible nation on Earth had flaws. We see the left trampling statues of them, labeling them racist for their poor judgment in regards to slavery. It is true, many of them owned slaves at a time when the entire world was trafficking in slavery. However, they had the vision to implement a system that could eradicate slavery through amendments. Many of them felt uncomfortable with slavery, but to change something that had existed in almost every major civilization in history would take time.

The British sent slaves all around the world. The Aztec Indians used prisoners of war as slaves. Egyptians enslaved the Jews. Even the Bible spoke of how to treat slaves. Our forefathers, in their amazing wisdom, planted the seeds for us to escape from the institution of enslaving each other. However, they did not have the strength to single-handedly end the institution and force a union of all the states.

We must not look down on them for their flaws. Even a great civil rights leader like Martin Luther King Jr. was accused of mistreating women. LGBTQ activist and leftist icon Ellen DeGeneres was accused of mistreating her staff. Bill Clinton mistreated an intern. J.K. Rowling suggested in a tweet that women menstruate, the outrage. We are all imperfect humans, and we should only reserve harsh judgment for those that break the law and hurt others.

So, while you may find flaws in Trump, you can find them in anyone. Even George Washington. The point is not inconsequential things people do on their worst days, but what they do at their best. Our nation was built at a time when kings and queens were thought to be the only way to rule people. George Washington could have used the army to claim himself king and disband the congress, but he did not because he believed in freedom. And he believed in the United States of America. For that, we should stand proudly when our national anthem plays in unison with one another as a group, not defined by our birthplace or skin color but our citizenship and belief in this country.

Two Qualities

There is no hidden agenda or shady modus operandi with Trump. You can read his Twitter feed if you are curious about his position on current events. He rarely stays silent. This is not politics as usual! It is far better than someone waiting for polling data and hiding behind speech writers to perfectly convey the most politically advantageous message. We might not all agree with everything he says, but at least we know where he stands. Communication is an important characteristic of great leadership.

Trump possesses two admirable qualities. First, he tries to do what he says he is going to do. Secondly, he does not back down from a fight. In leadership, it is important to follow through. Trump said he was going to build a wall and despite Democratic opposition and lukewarm Republican support, he built over 200 miles. The left's resistance is designed to make Trump look bad. If he came out tomorrow in favor of running water, they would be against it.

The Democrats' only goal is political power, which can be achieved by destroying Trump, and if America burns, it is acceptable collateral damage. They work tirelessly to come up with new ways to defeat his agenda. If Trump was a weak-minded man, he would surrender and give in to the raging mob. This would serve to embolden them and increase their blood lust. The left is a bully that intimidates and controls people through social shaming. The only way to counter a bully is with strength and resolve. Trump possesses both qualities and it leads him to success.

Listening to Tulsi Gabbard speak of the intimidation and coercion placed upon her when she entered Washington DC only reinforces this truth. Republicans can be just as coalesced, so focused on victory that they lose sight of what is best for our nation. These politicians become like plaque on the teeth. Every now and then we need to brush them away. Term limits on these establishment types are a great solution.

Trump never backs down from them. He has a spine, which is rare for Republicans. They usually cave quickly to the deranged hyperbolic media. The initial emotional gut reaction to a situation is not always the best time to make a law. It takes the confidence and strength of a true leader to stay on course. When the media starts twisting things for partisan advantage, he calls them out on it. Trump fearlessly calls them "fake news" to their face.

He does this by going as hard at the left as they go at the right. He is not afraid to counter-punch and dismisses their crazy demands. He is unaffected by "triggered feelings" or "safe spaces." He understands that this is just the beginning and eventually the emotional mob will turn on everyone. Negotiating with them is like negotiating with a terrorist. Give a little today, give a lot tomorrow.

Their goal is the destruction of American society. Perhaps they watched too many dystopian movies and want to create that lawless life where they can give into horrible instincts without consequence. It is irrational and ignorant. Hopefully, we do not have to get to the end of the road for enough people to see the stupidity. These people have been sold on a dream of utopia, but the real goal is Democratic political power.

The war Trump started was not with the rest of the world but with the elites. They are a powerful force in our society. People that look down on the rest of us from their ivory towers. People like Twitter CEO Jack Dorsey who thinks that feelings are more important than free speech. People like Sundar Pichai who thinks our Google searches should lead left. People like Susan Wojcicki who demonetizes conservative speech because she can. People like Mark Zuckerberg who believes in censoring a president. People like Jeff Bezos who thinks we should only buy what the WP is selling. People like David Brock who thinks Media Matters. People like George Soros who thinks chaos will usher in utopia. People like James Comey and Robert Muller who think everyday Americans are too unfit to pick a president. Therefore, investigations must be had undermining the will of the people.

Trump has a good vision for the country, but little political capital to spend. Most Democrats and Republicans in Washington despise him. They work daily to undermine him, and speak of him as a Neanderthal that is somehow less evolved. They have created a new bread of discrimination replacing orange with black. Anyone with such a self-righteous attitude in Washington is the fault of a half-asleep electorate willing to delude itself with propaganda.

To illustrate, look at how the Democrats acted toward Bill Bahar at his house judiciary committee hearing on July 28, 2020, it was indefensible. We must pay attention to our representatives. We cannot support legislators antagonizing and silencing the Attorney General while catering to an out of control Antifa mob.

Weak politicians who placate to the mob will not appease them, only embolden them. The bully will not stop asking for lunch money after getting paid. He will only ask for more and more. There is a time and place to stand up and fight. Trump has the personality to take them on in our interest. Democrats lack the character to stand with him. Their worst fear is giving Trump a victory, and not a civil war.

People want to call Trump mean but nice people make for weak leaders. Gerald Ford and Jimmy Carter were the nicest presidents but ineffective leaders. Great leaders stand up for what they believe in even if it offends everyone. A weak leader will change course easily. They will do the wrong thing to avoid stepping on toes. These types of politicians fester in our capital. They wave around like lilies in a hurricane. Trump is the only one to stand steady in the face of the opposition.

We are better off with a crass New Yorker than having a weak ineffective leader. Trump for all his media attention will never be the political genius Ronald Reagan was. Reagan ruled the world with sharp zingers. In the 1984 debate, he was questioned about being too old and said, "I will not make age an issue of this campaign. I am not going to exploit, for political purposes, my opponent's youth and inexperience," He won reelection in two sentences.

Reagan was harder to hate than Trump. He danced around liberals with effortless grace whereas Trump will run them over. Reagan had a much more impressive input (x) than Trump. However, they both got things done and stood up for our values and Constitution. Trump is more transparent than any president. Many view this as a flaw but it is a great attribute.

Trump's output (y) is arguably better than that of Reagan. Reagan did not want to over-stir the pot, Trump does not care. Trump is a skilled negotiator and has already made historic deals. In the end, history will look fondly upon both men. Years from now when the self-righteous minded Americans who spread divisive tribal politics become a relic of the past.

2

The Output of Trump (y)

The Trump Platform

Despite our human lust for the sensational, the planks of a political platform are the most important part of a candidate. The planks of a platform represent the 'vegetables' of what we should vote on. To be an informed consumers we must understand the argument and counter-argument on assorted variety of political topics. My support for President Trump centers around his platform (x), and his accomplishments (y). His agenda, when allowed to ripen, will bear fruit for all Americans.

Planks are the contracted agreement between the politician and the public. This is what you are going to do, this is why you are going to do it, and this is the effect it will have. We should make our choice for a candidate on two things: their platform and their willingness to fight for it. The purpose of the character argument is to make sure they will follow through with their promises. If a person like Joe Biden flip-flops around or is a serial liar, then what use is their platform? How can we entrust them to fulfill it?

He is not alone, most politicians are liars and sycophants to special-interest. They hide planks that can be extremely harmful to the general public but extremely helpful to their financial coffers. They are constantly moving goalposts for political convenience. Trump is not one of these politicians. Most of his political stances can be understood from very old interviews. For example, he went on Oprah Winfrey in 1988 and talked about making our allies pay their fair share.

A politician can lie to us all day about crowd sizes or what they ate for breakfast, but they better not lie about the direction they plan to take our country. These are the lies that matter. Like Obama, who ran as a pacifist opposed to the war in Iraq, then used our military in Afghanistan, Iraq, Syria, Libya, Yemen, Somalia, and Pakistan. His lie resulted in mass casualties and created a mess in the Middle East. It is worse than all 20,000 of Donald Trump's supposed lies combined.

My support for Trump centers around my belief in his platform because they are similar to mine. If brought to fruition, they will lead to a free and open society that is more prosperous and ripe with opportunity. Going after billionaires as Bernie Sanders suggests does not lead to less suffering. It leads to a short-term economic boost followed by a destroyed economic engine. The results are Venezuela because eventually, you run out of other people's money.

Trump may exaggerate things to make them more appealing, but he does not lie about his planks. No one doubts his sincerity in fulfilling his promises. Therefore, an earnest debate can be had about the planks. Will we be better off with more legal immigration and less illegal immigration? These are the types of important discussions we should be having.

Legal Immigration

It is tremendously unfair to force legal immigrants to wait in line for years to enter our country, while turning a blind eye to people that sneak across our borders or overstay their visas. We have designed a system to allow 1.1 million immigrants to enter our country every year. Just because more want to enter does not force us to allow them. Overpopulation has many negative side effects.

For instance, importing low-skilled workers will purloin the jobs that low-income Americans normally fill. This competition will produce unemployment and homelessness for people that desire work. It also drives wages down, because when an employer has a surplus of applicants and he can offer less.

Overpopulation will lead to more crime, and something that should alarm every Al Gore Liberal reading this, increased usage of fossil fuels. Americans use more fossil fuels per capital than any other nation on earth, therefore increasing our population would be an overall net positive to the world's carbon footprint. The same foot that hides in the closet and scares liberals at night.

To get back to the point, vital resources will be less available such as water, food, and medical treatment. Americans create more garbage than other country. Increasing our population will increase the amount of overall global pollution substantially.

Many people here do not realize how lucky they are. There is a good reason that so many people want to join our nation. We have amazing job opportunities, unparalleled freedoms, and wide-open spaces. We let more immigrants in than any other nation in the world. They make up about 14% of our overall population. We are exceptionally generous and yet the left hounds us constantly for not doing enough. They are insatiable.

A nation is merely a group of people working and living together under the laws they agree to self-impose. Thus, two important questions we should ask: Do you respect our freedoms? And will you work? Many countries around the globe do not respect our constitutional amendments. Specifically, freedom of religion, freedom of speech, and the right to bear arms.

In China, they enslaved a Muslim minority population and sentenced them to concentration camps. They have little respect for people that think or look different. They have a virus based fear of black people and almost no Black or Caucasian citizens. There is no such thing as freedom of speech or the right to bear arms in China.

In the Middle East, many Muslim countries persecute Christian minorities. In other countries, the Muslims denounce other Muslims. The hostilities over religion are as old as society itself. America was one of the first countries to provide a religious sanctuary to Pilgrims and Puritans. Many of these countries are intolerant of outside religion.

Great Britain and Canada have limitations on "hate speech." James Sears, a Canadian editor of a newspaper in Toronto, was jailed for saying hateful things about women and Jews. While we should all disagree with everything he said, putting him in jail only makes him look like a martyr for free speech and gives his cause more publicity. He said his words were meant satirically. The simple truth is nobody should be in jail for saying things unless we can show direct harm, feelings not included.

The real danger in this limitation on free speech is that they can manipulate it to silence anyone who disagrees. Label someone a racist and suddenly their speech is hate. It is a tactic that big tech constantly uses on social media platforms. A way to silence people that think on the other side of the political spectrum.

Many countries like Britain do not respect our 2nd amendment. In 1997, Britain prohibited most guns, and to this day, rarely allow police officers to carry. Ironically, the murder rate has surpassed the pre-gun prohibition period. Stricter gun laws did nothing to curve homicides. Knife attacks are at record levels. The problem of gun violence needs to be solved with methods other than stricter laws on law-abiding citizens. Considering most criminals do not know or abide by gun laws.

While we may not want to allow people we disagree with to speak, we must not stop them. That is the American way. People from other nations that do not respect our laws will bring the same mental traps that led them to flee their home country. We must keep the promise of our forefather's Constitution bright.

The Wall

Liberal elites lecture us on how ineffective walls are while surrounding their homes with walls. They are smart enough to know the effect of a wall, and that is why they want to stop their construction. If walls were useless, they would negotiate DACA for it. Giving up something "useless" to get something meaningful. However, they refuse to do this for two reasons. First, they do not want to give Trump a victory. Second, immigrants overwhelmingly vote Democratic.

The payoff is simple: immigrants get more immigration and welfare assistance, and Democrats get more votes. As usual, Democrats do not care about the effect it has on the country as a whole because they are safely tucked away in their fortress. They want to energize the base by focusing on the emotional input of helping the "underdog."

Democrats fight Trump tooth and nail to get illegal immigrants counted on the 2020 census. Why? To get more representation in places like California so they can shift the electoral college. It is like a version of Jerry-maundering, but instead of moving district lines around, you move massive amounts of people. Specifically, people from other countries into our country, then count them on the census and give them a path to citizenship and the right to vote. It is a political tactic designed for political power. So far, non-citizens can vote in eleven different local elections around the country.

If we have designed our country such that people fill out a form and wait in line to enter, then yes, of course, we should lock the backdoor. If you want more immigrants in our country, then take your appeal to the American public, convince them to convince legislators, and create new laws that allow more people in the front door. We need to debate the questions because a country is merely a collection of people, and if you change the people, you change the country.

How many people should we allow to enter per year? What does the endgame of the Democratic playbook look like? Of the 7.6 billion people on earth, how many of them would want to become US citizens? What if we offered free healthcare, universal income, free college tuition, head start, child care, SNAP, welfare, food stamps, housing assistance, security income program, childcare, social security, and free transportation? How many of the 3 billion people around the globe who live on $2.50 or less per day might want to come here? Billions? Suddenly we go from a country of 330 million to 4.5 billion. How can we fit all these people? Would our economy collapse from the influx of unskilled labor? The education cost alone would bankrupt us.

We have to quell our emotions and draw the line somewhere. The rest of the world would be a ghost town, and our country would be overwhelmed with people from different cultures. If having this many people is a good thing, why is China trying to reduce their population? Could you imagine all the waste? All the different languages? Whose culture would dominate? Various intolerant religious beliefs living so close would surely lead to violence. Idle people who cannot find work would begin robbing stores for food. It is a horrible idea and would result in a despotic mess. Yet, the left pushes for it because immigrants tend to vote Democratic. Republicans push for it because businesses want cheaper labor.

Unlike the elitist in both parties, Trump's goals are clear and specific, and he works tirelessly to achieve them. He said he wants to build a wall, and what does he do? He tries his best to build it. Congress does not cooperate. Federal judges block him, so he circumvents them and uses the pentagon. He never gives up, despite all the negative forces.

Now the Democrats try to downplay it and say much of it is a replacement, which is great because it needed to be replaced. Or they say he didn't complete it. Which is true, because they stopped him. He is not a king, nor should he be. We live in a representative democracy with checks and balances. If he failed to build the wall, it is because we as a nation failed him. We failed him by sending irrational idiotic people to Washington.

Trump continues to fight but he doesn't jail the federal judge in Texas that blocked his wall construction. To somehow claim this is a failure is hopelessly misleading and manipulative. The only way Trump fails is if he gives up. If Trump had his way, he would complete the wall tomorrow. Especially when it is something that is in our national interest. We spend billions and billions of dollars on subs that rarely see the light of day or over $700 billion every year on welfare programs that create more dependents. Why not put up a wall for $10 billion with a big door to keep people from running across our border? The most ridiculous arguments have been used against the wall.

Trump says he is going to have Mexico pay for it, and he renegotiates NAFTA so that Mexico's trade imbalance is corrected. This brings in additional revenue to the United States, which can in turn be used to build the wall. The truth behind his promise has yet to penetrate the outrage mob. They still mock his statements.

Meanwhile, Joe Biden tells factory workers he is going to stand up for them in Washington, then votes for NAFTA and TPP. This causes millions of jobs to be sent overseas. This one lie is more consequential than any of the 20,000 the media accuses Trump of. To add insult to injury, Biden tells coal miners, learn to code.

Trump does what he says he's going to do, which is rare for a politician. Normally they say one thing on the campaign trail, then cave to special interest once they get to Washington DC. Trump's failure to comply with this orthodoxy drives the bureaucratic elites crazy. Frustrated, that they cannot buy him off. They seek to demonize him at every turn. These groups that represent large multinational corporations often have a special interest that can be harmful to the general interest of Americans.

Trumpanomics

Amazingly, Trump has been able to accomplish anything, given the level of vitriol thrown at him. His opposition is so ripe with anger that they cannot even coherently explain why they oppose him. Perhaps it is because he has an impressive list of accomplishments to tout, including the economy.

Trump continues to fight trade imbalances. Allowing for American manufacturers to compete on a global scale. Our companies are at a competitive disadvantage because they pay a decent wage. In Asia, they can pay pennies on the dollar for the same work; using child labor, eighty-hour workweeks, and offering no benefits. It is a modern-day version of slavery, with many people unable to afford basic-necessities after working all week in harsh conditions.

Exploiting cheap labor weakens us by reducing the number of American jobs. The only advantage of such a system is the bottom line of corrupt corporations. Politicians are paid off through lobbyists, and bills get pushed through congress. The American people do not pay attention because they are distracted by the advertisements. Large shoe companies spend millions on making themselves out to be social justice warriors while running female sweatshops in Vietnam.

If you want to ship jobs around the world, there is an argument to be had for the decent treatment of workers that produce our goods. We should not be left wondering if a pair of sneakers was made by a young Asian girl making $0.23 per hour, then sold to Americans for $205 per shoe so that a corporation can have record earnings. Let's just stop doing it.

The strategy is simple. Pay a few million dollars to politicians and celebrities, or pay hundreds of millions in wages to American workers. Trump is a threat to these corporate giants, and they hate him for it. He cannot be bought by them, and this drives a lot of the wealthy Anti-Trump sentiment in this country. They want to tear down Trump to protect their scheme.

Social justice warriors claiming to be against oppression and islamophobia turn a blind eye to all the human rights violations China commits. Including something that sounds like a conspiracy theory but is not; countless articles speak of them, organ harvesting the aforementioned Islamic slaves. There are many other alleged human rights violations by China, all ignored by the globalist social justice warriors of the left.

Unlike Joe Biden, Trump stands up to China. He imposed tariffs on them in response to their forced technology transfer, intellectual property theft, and chronically abusive trade practices. China, whose strength grew from our greed. American corporations are eager to exploit low labor costs shipped millions of jobs to them. This happened by corporations joining forces with a political class willing to sell legislation for campaign contributions. Add an asleep electorate and we end up with millions of wages pumped into a communist country. They are the world's new supervillain with their demented views on freedom.

Trump took a pro-military stance on the campaign trail and has secured a record funding of $716 billion per year. He also improved the contribution from our NATO allies. They are now spending $69 billion more on defense than in 2016. No longer are we the military police for all of Europe but in a competent alliance with a worthy partner that can help us tide the evil empires. Countries such as China, Russia, Iran, and North Korea that lust for global domination. Soon that could transform into a lust for intergalactic domination.

Foreseeing this, Trump began a new 6th branch of the Armed services known as the Space Force. Mocked by liberals but it will be his lasting legacy. Future generations will colonize far off planets, and they will do it using the Trump Force. The most ironic twist of all this is that Trump will be revered as one of the greatest presidents in history.

Reductions in taxation freed up billions of dollars to be invested in businesses and grow the economy. Millions of more Americans working led to 3.9 million people being lifted off food stamps and America's unemployment rate had dropped below 4%. We were seeing some of the best numbers in the last 50 years.

Trump accomplished this by opening up ANWR and approving the Keystone XL and Dakota Access Pipelines. Two things Obama refused to do. Our oil production reached an all-time high which reduced our dependence on OPEC. Energy independence is no small thing. It is the reason we are less engaged in the Middle East. America has increased coal exports by 60%. Let alone, the United States is a net natural gas exporter for the first time since the 1950s.

Trump said he would cut taxes and deregulate the bureaucracy, then signed the biggest tax cut and reform bills in US history. He withdrew from the job-killing Paris Climate Accord. Canceled the anti-coal so-called Clean Power Plan. Reached a breakthrough agreement with the E.U. to increase U.S. exports. Imposed tariffs on foreign steel and aluminum to protect our national security. He replaced the NAFTA deal with the USMCA trade deal to balance trade in North America.

Consequently causing a surge in the GDP to over 3% for four quarters of his administration. The stock market increased and job growth surged to record levels before being derailed by the pandemic. Something the Democrats are trying to pin on him. This is an overreach and insults our intelligence, only a political hack would blame Trump for the China Virus.

Trump used executive action to eliminate the Obamacare individual mandate penalty. This was a tax on young, healthy people designed to subsidize older people's healthcare. Should one group of people be forced to pay for another group's healthcare? When first starting out in life. things can be difficult. Putting unwanted taxation on young people is wrong.

The thought behind it is they will be paid back. But why should anyone buy into this system? What guarantees do we have? Tomorrow's politicians could collapse it without warning. Are we supposed to blindly trust the government? This is the disastrous thinking behind social security, and the reason older people are deadly serious about it. They spent their lives paying into a system that can be changed or gutted at any time. It is quite nerve-racking to have that much money tied up in a government institution. It is not fair. We should have never taken their money in the first place.

To mitigate the cost of healthcare, the Trump Administration is using association health plans, short-term duration plans, and approving affordable generic drugs. They also reformed Medicare to stop hospitals from overcharging low-income seniors on drugs. Not to mention, Trump signed the Right-To-Try legislation, which allows people with life-threatening conditions to try experimental medicines. He also signed legislation to hold the VA Accountable for veterans' healthcare.

Conservative Appointments

Who can forget the Brett Kavanaugh hearing? Liberals were so upset screaming bloody murder in the streets. Funny how all that emotion just dissipated. The country did not change all that much since his appointment. Wealth redistribution was not ruled unconstitutional. A woman's right to vote was not undermined. However, we did see how far the political smear machine of the left is willing to go. They did it all for partisan gain. The calculus was simple. Put an innocent man on trial for his "bad" politics.

Kamala Harris had her mind made up before any facts could get out. She believed the unsubstantiated claims of an accuser with no corroboration and clear motive to destroy a man of differing political views. Not only was there no evidence of a crime, but there was contradictory evidence to the crime. To give Kamala credit, she believed Joe Biden's accusers as well. However, that was back in the primary when it was in her political interest. After joining the ticket Biden transformed back to innocent. Funny how guilt and innocence always seem to align with her political allegiances.

With the blaring intense media headlights, this show trial created such a stir of emotion in the American populace that innocent until proven guilty was overturned. Celebrities chanted, 'I'm with her.' There was not one provable fact that ever came out of any of the stories. Our speculation into a story without facts is frivolous, and we certainly cannot convict someone based on hearsay. Our prisons would overflow. Imagine the power of being able to send someone to jail based on a simple accusation.

The sketchy details of the accusations lacked a specific location. That is a pretty basic fact. Especially, if it will be brought in front of the entire nation under partisan suspicion. It was a media circus full of poignant story telling. The left rejoiced in all their interconnected emotional outrage. The sacrifice of an innocent man was inconsequential.

Anyone who was accused under such murky conditions should feel angry at an injustice system. However, Brett kept his cool as the trial played out in the media where there are no rules. When Ford gave her testimony, it was more about conveying emotion than giving facts. She was probably coached on how to "properly" cry. She allowed herself to be a political pawn.

By confirming more circuit court judges than any other new administration, Trump has put faithful jurists on the bench, including two Supreme Court Justices in Brett Kavanaugh and Neil Gorsuch. This prevents a wild liberal Supreme Court from radically interpreting some of our laws and creating tyranny for Americans.

With great respect and condolences to Supreme Court Judge Ruth Bader Ginsburg, who passed away on September 18, 2020, Trump will have the ability to add another Justice. Hopefully he will pick a truly conservative jurist such as Amy Coney Barrett. In theory it should be a simple transition, however in reality it will be bedlam.

3

The Hatred of Trump (x)

Opposition to Trump

The adversarial hatred for Trump centers around egregious predictions that if were true no one would support him. They accuse him of being a horrible input (x) that after being sent to the White House (f(x)) would output (y) cringe worthy things. They predict he will usher in a new era of slavery, harm immigrants, or stomp on women's rights. However, none of this is true, the moment we realize that is the moment we support him. Therefore, the left is in a fever pitch to feed their narratives and keep people believing in all their horrible predictions.

He's a nationalist!

Trump puts American interest ahead of other nations because he works for America. The media labels him as a nationalist and tries to turn this into a smear. If our president does not represent our interest, then what nation does he represent?

The alternative to this would be a globalist or someone that represents the interest of other nations over that of America. This is like hiring a lawyer that represents the interest of society over that of a client. It sounds noble, but it is useless to the accused. Who would ever want a lawyer that does not represent their interest?

Our president should find compromises on common sense global strategies but when there are competing interests, he should push for America first. This strategy maintains our power on the world stage. While America is not perfect, we are a fair country that values freedom. For the most part, world peace rests on our shoulders.

Giving up our power could lead to a despotic regime consuming the world. Consequently, endangering future generations leading to death and slavery. Anyone that thinks America is irredeemable has no grasp of history. Texts are littered with evil civilizations slaughtering for "difference hatred." Therefore, we must stand for justice but also maintain our interest which is peace and prosperity.

Leaders should represent their nation's best interests. This is the fundamental principle of being a nation. Our leaders sit down with other leaders and make decisions that can affect our everyday lives. Do we want those negotiations to go against our interests? Or in the interest of some unattainable noble truth? Barack Obama espouses about. Of course, we want a strong principled proponent of our interest.

It's all Trump's fault!

There is a simple principle in business, "the buck stops here." Good business owners take full responsibility for all aspects of their company. If something should happen to an employee, then the boss must act. If he does not, then he must assume part of the responsibility. This is a valid principle because the boss of a company is an authoritarian. In most states, he can fire at will for any reason. While he cannot stop everything, he can make a climate that lacks harassment. He does have tools to use if he so chooses.

This principle is valid for business and not politics. The left cannot start a dumpster fire and use the "buck stops here" principal against Trump's America. By way of example, with the virus. Democratic governors push for lockdowns that slow down the economy. Then they blame Trump for a slow economy. Trump is not a king. He cannot fire Nancy Pelosi. The Democrats have power, and they are using it to muddy the waters and create a chaotic mess, then blame Trump for the economic disaster.

He's divisive!

How dare liberals blame Donald Trump for being divisive when they hold a shiv covered in racist epithets. The victim of the stabbing is not to blame for the anger of the perpetrator. This crime falls squarely on the shoulders of those that have been airing hateful Hitler filled rhetoric. Lobbing wild claims with absolutely zero evidence, it is destructive.

*Trump killed 190,000 Americans!**

This section was censored.

Internet trolls are running rampant through cyberspace labeling Donald Trump, the virus killer. That message has spread to the elite in Washington as their official talking point. What motive would Trump have for spreading the virus? The economic engine of America was roaring back to life. Our reaction to this virus has caused unrest and slowed the recovery. The virus has been bad for both America and Trump.

Hard to believe Democrats are using this as a political weapon. John Kerry never used 9/11 against George W. Bush. Nobody foresaw this virus except maybe Bill Gates. There was no manual on how to stop it. Even looking back on what we could have done differently, there are few answers. Blaming 190,000 deaths on Donald Trump is not a solution. It is a disgusting partisan tool used by a former president against a sitting president. It is indefensible and will destroy Obama's legacy for future generations. Sewing division for political gain shows the illness of a partisan. Unhinged and fighting for victory at all costs has its drawbacks. For all his faults, at least Bush had the decency to sit back and let his successor govern.

The real question is: what would Democrats have done differently? Wait longer to close our borders? They resisted Trump's initial travel ban. Mandated a nationwide lockdown for months on end. California has been the most locked-down state in the union, and yet they still have the most cases.

In June of 2018 on his HBO show Real Time, Bill Maher said, "Can I ask about the economy because this economy is going pretty well? I feel like the bottom has to fall out at some point. And by the way, I'm hoping for it. Because I think one way you get rid of Trump is a crashing economy. So, please, bring on the recession. Sorry if that hurts people, but it's either root for a recession or you lose your democracy,"

Enemy of the People

The fake news media is ground zero for the radical hatred of Trump. Hyperpolarized by the audacity of a nation to elect a president that does not bend to their will. They label normal things he does as "disqualifying" or "unpresidential." Then they turn to the American people like angry snobs saying, "See, he did it again!" When his supporters continue to support him, they get frustrated and amplify their rhetoric to indefensible proportions.

Trump is just offensive enough to annoy the opposition, but not so offensive that he alienates his base. He keeps the fire going and gets maximum exposure while turning leftists into angry little villains. They sit around on panels with eight people and one point of view, bashing him over idiotic things like wrestling videos. They do not realize that they are draining their credibility and destroying their integrity.

In a perfect world, Trump's political adversaries would remain respectful only disagreeing on matters of policy. However, we do not live in this world! Democratic operatives have infiltrated our media at the highest level to spread this hatred. They have brainwashed people for political power. These American voters have become hostile to any type of intervention. A group so entrenched in mass psychosis facts become an annoyance. To keep the herd in line, they perform sacrifices. All too often, the outrage mob turns on liberal mayors and celebrities. No one is safe.

This brand of irrational groupthink has been responsible for some of the worst atrocities in human history. The left is playing a dangerous game that they cannot control. Ostracizing people who think differently is a terrible precedent to build politics on because you can never be "woke" enough. Today, it's OK to go after MAGA hat-wearing white kids, but tomorrow it could be white liberal women. This type of bullying is unjust. As reasonable Americans, we must do our best to end it.

The press should be a neutral referee in this left-right dichotomy. Both sides of the political spectrum need to be held accountable. Nobody wins when the referees cheat. We see them walking into the "left's" locker room. Could you imagine if a referee made horrible calls, then walked into the opponent's locker room to celebrate with them after the game? The left is so bent on winning they overlook it, but we all lose in the end.

Trump stands up to these villains, and they hate him so much for it. They would allow innocent people to die if it meant Trump would suffer politically. Notably, in Seattle, the mayor chose to allow dangerous anarchy and chaos reign in the city streets. An autonomous zone was created with the sole intent of anarchy. Borders "walls" were erected, armed criminals "policed" the streets, properties were vandalized, radicals yelled slogans, and Mayor Jenny Durkan called it "the summer of love."

She intentionally told officers to stand down and allowed a police precinct to be vandalized and destroyed. Trump offered federal assistance and asked that local law enforcement be allowed to do their job. Of course, once Trump chose a side, the Democratic mind immediately took the opposite. This tactic led to the loss of two young black lives. Their blood is on the hands of Jenny Durkan and her incompetent leadership. She may have thought she won a political battle against the president, but all she did was remove the police safeguards in place to preserve innocent life.

The protest mob needs to be reined in by strong politicians. A rational thinking mayor would never allow people to take over city blocks when she could deploy the police to stop it. Refusing to use the police should be made unlawful. A politically weak-minded person paralyzed by the mob on one side and her Anti-Trumpism on the other. Her actions should be criminal.

As much blame as she deserves, everyone who voted for her deserves blame. They created a toxic mess with their high and mighty intentions. Until these Democrat-run cities are handed over to Republicans, the populace will suffer. Then after a honeymoon period, Republicans will become corrupt, and they should return to the Democrats. This is how a system achieves balance.

Politicians are supposed to spin stories, not journalists. They did this after Trump called members of the notorious MS-13 gang "animals." The media intentionally omitted the context of MS-13 to suggest he meant all immigrants. The free press! Spinning a story to nail the sitting President of the United States. What kind of world are we living in?

Freedom of the press is vital; we must welcome dissent especially in politics. The left aggressively tries to shut down conservatives. Fox news journalists are under constant pressure from leftist. Bill O'Reilly was forced out of the No Spin Zone and Alex Jones was banned from social media platforms. Steve Bannon was charged with fraud. Now they have their sights set on Tucker Carlson. They obsess over how to cancel him. They use Twitter mobs to boycott his advertisers and dox his family. Forcing him to move after Antifa members showed up at his house and threatened his wife.

These people are enemies of our Constitution, specifically the first, second, and fourth amendments. They do not belong in our country. They hate people for supporting a duly elected president. Dissent is healthy, however, disrespect is counterproductive and only serves to divide our people. It must end.

RUSSIA RUSSIA RUSSIA

Trump is a man elected by the will of the people, and instead of bowing gracefully, partisans continue to fight for impeachment. It began with the Russian Hacking-Colluding story. This fits the Clinton campaign narrative that Trump is dangerous, specifically by being under the thumb of Russian President Vladimir Putin—apparently blackmailed by a salacious scandal. The only problem with this "leftist fairy tale," is the fact that there is no credible evidence for it. The only fact is a partial, debunked, shady dossier cooked up in a foreign country, paid for by the Democratic opposition, and sold to the FBI.

Comey's spying on an opposing campaign at the behest of his appointee and co-conspirator Barack Obama will go down in history as one of the most egregious sins of our democracy. Unacceptable under any circumstance. It was a partisan witch hunt with zero integrity. If Russian collusion warranted an investigation, then non-partisans should have conducted it without reproach.

In this case, there should have never been an investigation because there was no crime. Justice requires us to adhere to a simple principle: evidence of a crime before an investigation of a crime. Instead, this was an investigation looking for a crime. The shady dossier does not stand as evidence as a simple investigation into it would reveal its source was the Hillary Clinton Campaign.

Senator Lindsey Graham's newly released documents reveal a similar scenario played out for the Clinton Campaign. Namely concerns over foreign interference within her campaign. However, the FBI took a dramatically different approach. She was told and given time to fire or reprimand the people involved.

The partisan hacks at the FBI did not give Trump the same respect. The Obama appointed anti-Trump bureaucracy shamelessly used shady evidence to spy on Trump. The effect subverted the election and tarnished the political capital of Trump. They branded him as unfit for office and launched the Muller investigation. A dark cloud loomed over our great nation for years to come, with sensational reports being dripped to the media. It all amounted to nothing. However, we have not held the liberal media mob accountable.

Obama will go down in history as the only sitting US president to ever spy on an opposing party's candidate. If one is willing to cross that red-line, one must have legitimate evidence. This heavy-handed tactic of using FBI informants to spy on a campaign has no place in the United States of America. Obama was a weak president unable to stand-up to the voices of the far left. Our founding fathers would roll over in their graves if they had witnessed these banana republic antics.

At least Richard Nixon did not appoint a partisan hack to head the FBI, then use him to dig up dirt on a political opponent. Until the people of the left hold their political class accountable, they will continue to act with corruption. Hopefully, the independents will not support them, and their political power will vanish. Unless our republic has become too corrupt and people too blind to stand up for what is right.

Included in the Russia debacle was the obstruction of justice charge. The notion that President Trump fired FBI director James Comey to cover up a crime has no basis in reality because there was no crime. The only crime was when Comey leaked to a professor who leaked to the media, which led to the appointment of special prosecutor Robert Mueller. Mueller created a dangerous thing, a team of partisan lawyers in search of a crime.

The raiding of Trump's lawyer Michael Cohen's office was a dark day in our democracy. Our founding fathers created the fourth amendment to stop these types of investigations—overzealous prosecutor desperate to make convictions sifting through attorney-client privileged information. It has no place in America, and yet the brainwashed partisans support it.

Trump leaves just enough breadcrumbs to rile up the left into overreaching for evidence. They sacrifice the rule of law for an attempt at revenge. The investigation was not up to par and when it was time to investigate the investigators, the Inspector General said, 27 department cell phones were "accidentally wiped." Is this standard protocol or obstruction of justice? Shouldn't we maintain all the evidence surrounding such a high-level investigation?

Attacking from all angles, partisans used the emoluments clause of the US Constitution to sue the president and threaten impeachment because foreign nationals stayed at the Trump International Hotel. This is beyond the spirit of the law. Our founding fathers designed this part of the Constitution for foreign governments trying to buy political influence over our leaders. They did not design it to prevent Jimmy Carter's brother from running a peanut farm while he was president.

The lawsuit proceeded under the ruling of U.S. District Judge Peter J. Messitte in Maryland. The claim was that Trump's hotel had an unfair advantage over the competition, despite Trump putting his assets in a revocable trust overseen by his eldest son and chief financial officer.

Do we believe some Kuwaiti oil tycoon is getting special favors for staying at a hotel? What evidence is there? Because that is what you would need, evidence. Trump's wife and children cannot even control his Twitter habit— and yet some Muslim Cleric is staying at a hotel getting presidential room service? Isn't Trump Islamophobic? Only a partisan hack could think he is profiteering off the presidency. Everything is a fair-market transaction. This lawsuit is just an attempt to use a loophole to unseat a duly elected president.

Then there is the preposterous 25th amendment argument. Our government designed it in the wake of President John F Kennedy's assassination to transfer power. They designed its use for physical impairments, not as a partisan tool to impeach someone you disagree with politically. It is disheartening to see so many psychologists violate the Goldwater Rule which states that they are not to diagnose someone with a mental disease unless they have met with that person. One of them wrote an entire book about how dangerous he was. What harm came from Trump? These mental health professionals need to pause and reflect, perhaps they are the ones causing harm. Scaring children and easily influenced people by labeling the president of the United States a horrible mentally ill person. They create panic then blame the panic they created on Trump.

Instead of impeachment, the better course of action is to have a civilized debate. One where only the facts and issues are at play. Branding people as racist or mentally unfit is not a good political strategy. It is a codependent cycle: lazy politician, ignorant citizen, and yellow journalist.

Poor journalism is disconcerting, but our focus should be on the consumers of media. A television show will only go as far as the ratings allow it. When people tune out, the show ends. Ultimately, the media are not to blame; it is the consumers of the media. If they are under-educated, gullible, and easily manipulated, then they will keep buying the propaganda, no matter the cost

Race Relations

Our race is a social construct manipulated by the left for political gain. They once used it to rally white people against black people. Now they rally black people against white people. Over what? Race is something we created in our collective heads to simplify the world into five color-coated categories; yellow, black, brown, white, and red. However, the genetic diversity of humans does not neatly line up with these four categories. It is an overtly racist system designed to separate us into tribes and have us fight so that Democrats can energize their political base and gain power.

In early America, racist white Democrats used skin color to enslave blacks. The racist south divided people into tribal camps and made up horrible lies about blacks. They used it to motivate their base and suppress the rights of blacks. They called black people untamed and warned if we released them, they would riot in the streets and burn down our cities.

Then a Republican came along named Abraham Lincoln, who said all men were created equal. He was the first Republican president, a group founded on abolishing slavery. A group that fought and died in a civil war to unchain Americans. To this day they are the only political party pushing for a color blind society.

Racist Democrats are trying to undo the civil rights legislation in California that prevents discrimination based on race. Because now they want to discriminate against Asians and Caucasians. Thus, they are still the party of racists, but now it is against light skinned people. Why do we get so lost in skin color? It is terrible.

Imagine a world where people could take a pill to change their race. It's not so far off. A pill that could somehow increase or decrease the melanin in the skin. Suppose someone stood before us and presented as black, despite being born white. Do they qualify for reparations? Affirmative action? Protected class membership? Can they drop n-bombs?

What about the reverse scenario? If a person went from black to white. Would they now automatically become racist? Would they have white privilege? Would their heritage change? Would their oppression level change? Should we treat them differently? Would they act differently?

These are all important questions. The answers matter. Do you believe that skin color alone makes someone a different person? Does their personality matter? Down this road is a divisive evil that will cause civil unrest. We must treat each other equally in the eyes of the law.

Recently, there has been a rash of racially motivated prosecutions. White civilians acting in self-defense accused of homicide. One such case appears to be Jake Gardner, the owner of The Hive bar in Omaha, Nebraska. The incident occurred in the wake of the George Floyd protest and from what we know in the video footage it appears he was slammed to the ground and fired a warning shot. The original "peaceful protester" ran off. Then another man came up from behind him and put him in a choke-hold. He claimed to have given warning and when the guy would not let go he shot in self-defense.

How can a man be charged for homicide after being put in a choke-hold on the ground? No one has the right to assault anyone. Being left unconscious on the sidewalk during a riot is life-threatening. Anyone that says otherwise is a racist, like the DA in this case. He is trying to please an angry mob by sacrificing the rule of law. This headline is the reason for the prosecution: White man kills mostly peaceful black protester.

Why do we fixate on skin color so much? What if it was about eye color instead? What if we thought brown-eyed people were superior? What if green-eyed people enslaved blue-eyed people who lived under the boot of the brown-eyed people? When the blue-eyed people were finally free would they turn around and want revenge on the brown-eyed people?

Two wrongs do not make a right. What racist whites did to blacks was wrong, and trying to correct it by discriminating against another group of people is wrong. We are all unique individuals and those that seek to segregate us based on our skin tone are immoral and repugnant no matter the reason. Color blind is the only truth.

Is Trump a racist?

What if Trump took the pill and became black? Would the left still consider him racist? When did this narrative begin? The left-wing media machine branded Trump a racist, sexist, and xenophobe, the day he decided to run for president. But what has he done to deserve it since becoming president? Before the virus, these groups were thriving under his leadership. He pushed for deregulation and tax breaks that led to GDP and stock market growth. Which led to better-paying jobs for all Americans.

The racist label is considered an acceptable political tactic because it works. Once a victim is labeled racist, they are left helplessly trying to prove a negative. What can you say back? "I have black friends." This weak response will be mocked by the left as they pounce. "I donated to BLM," nobody cares. This only shows a wokeness to the label and allows them to dominate.

The best response was by Joan Rivers to Darcus Howe. She said, "I just went NUTS!" after being accused of racism, "I stopped the whole show, and just SCREAMED at him: 'How dare you! I am not a racist!' I demanded an apology. I stopped the whole show until he finally said he was sorry."

Do we have to take these extreme measures to get people to stop abusing the word? Trying to score cheap political points by causally labeling someone as unacceptable. They slap someone down with a label then watch them topple over. Maybe they think that they are playing a video game. It is the audience that must disavow it. We must turn our backs on anyone that casually uses it. When it is used we must demand evidence. It disrespects generations of blacks who suffered mightily by true racist. Getting lukewarm coffee at Starbucks is not equivalent to being whipped by an angry racist who thinks you are subhuman.

We give far to much credit to accusations. People that accuse others of sexual assault, child abuse, racism, or homophobia are tarred and feathered for life. We as a society must reserve judgement until all the facts have come out. We are the ones that give power to these bitter rivals often times with a political ax to grind.

In May 2016, the Clinton Campaign attempted to brand Trump as "Dangerous Donald." While the name did not stick, the narrative did, and to this day a significant portion of our population believes our president to be dangerous. They believe him to be a Racist-Fascist-Sexist-Xenophobic-Hitler. Why? Because the Clinton Campaign poured millions into the idea, and the mainstream media echoed it.

This false narrative brainwashed ordinary citizens into zombies chanting, "Trump is a racist." Yet, there is no factual basis for his racism. There is no hidden email where he plans to reintroduce slavery or segregation. There is no N-bomb tape.

However, evidence to the contrary exists. His first scripted TV appearance was on The Jeffersons. He appeared on the Fresh Prince of Bel-Air with Will Smith. Also, he appeared on Oprah Winfrey's show multiple times and is friends with Mike Tyson and Herschel Walker. He used to get name-dropped in rap songs. He did the Hotline Bling dance on SNL. These are not the actions of a racist man.

Racist people do racist things and he has done nothing racist since becoming president. In fact, he has met with many black leaders and artists like Kanye West and Martin Luther King III to address concerns in the black community. In his 40 plus years of public life, no one with any credibility ever considered him racist. It was not until he ran for president as a Republican that the racist narrative amplified to indefensible proportions. Despite this, there is no penalty for those who push the false narrative. They still write articles in their fancy papers pretending to have credibility.

To Trump's credit, he lured them in just the right way, by offering a quote which, when mentioned out of context, would lead to the false assumption. "We're taking people out of the country. You wouldn't believe how bad these people are. These aren't people. These are animals." Trump was speaking of MS-13 gang members. These are not people worth defending, and yet the leftist hierarchy does it just to defy the president.

It is not surprising, especially after they took his famous quote out of context, "When Mexico sends its people, they're not sending their best... They're sending people that have lots of problems... They're bringing drugs. They're bringing crime. They're rapists. And some, I assume, are good people."

Who can disagree? Cartel members are crossing our border and wreaking havoc on some of our communities. They traffic humans and smuggle drugs. We must target these people and defeat them. The outrage stems from a broad brush painted by the media. They transformed what Trump said into, "all immigrants are drug dealers and rapists." Did he ever mention how many are good people and how many are criminals? Is it wrong to put a spotlight on rapists?

The media accused Trump of having supporters who were racist. Guilt by association, the only problem is unlike Joe Biden, Trump never associated himself with these racist. Because he has racist supporters does not make him racist. Jake Tapper tried to show a fake connection between Trump and right-wing extremist, David Duke. Why is our media foaming at the mouth to bring down this president?

They cringed for months over his Charlottesville comments, "Yes, I think there's blame on both sides." Again who can disagree with this? There is blame on both sides. Unite the Right organizer Jason Kessler applied for the permit from the City of Charlottesville. This is a very important detail most people in the media ignored.

When someone decides to have a protest, it is Un-American to have a counter-protest. We are a nation of free speech and no matter how deplorable the point of view, we must allow it to be expressed. The counter-protest movement must be denounced universally by everyone. When BLM decides to peacefully protest nobody should ever try to stop them with a counter-protest. This sets a terrible precedent.

After fights broke out on both sides, the leftest were chanting "bleed, Nazi, bleed" after a man was knocked to the ground. A mob that included Antifa hit him with bats and sticks and he was hurt badly. Denying his humanity deserves blame. Over thirty people were injured on both sides.

On the Unite the Right side there were nasty racist people carrying Nazi paraphernalia and yelling obnoxious obscenities. They were starting fights and cursing at people. Most tragically a woman lost her life to a deranged motorist. There was blame on both sides.

His other statement was that there were "very fine people on both sides," which again is true. There were many respected journalists from both sides covering the protest. Also, there was a conservative woman that the NY Times wrote a positive story about. Her group was not racist, just wanted to preserve history.

The whole thing got twisted into Donald Trump supports white supremacists, despite the fact that he denounced them, as I denounce them, as America denounces them. But we must always defend their right to protest.

They are a weak organization, their only source of strength is racist liberals. Groups that want to overturn anti-discrimination laws in California only embolden a counter whit racist movement. We must push for a color blind narrative as the division will only lead to massive suffering. Minorities have suffered enough in our country.

Most leftest promised Jim Crow if we elected Trump, but we have had no such thing. No "tribes" have suffered under his leadership. They have all flourished. The unemployment numbers of minority groups are the lowest ever recorded.

What has happened is a new breed of "acceptable racism" has sprung up in places like Freedom, Georgia. Billed as a black-only community. Imagine trying to buy a house there as a white person. Would you be discriminated against? Would people at the grocery store give you funny looks like you invaded their safe space?

The left has ushered in a new brand of racism against Donald Trump. Let's call it orangist. Their tone is similar to that of old racist slaveholders talking about black people. They speak of how vile he is like a subhuman pig swallowing around in his orangeness. They go on about him being a menace threatening the lives of immigrants by instituting travel bans. Replace the colors and they sound like old articles in the New York Times, "NEGRO COCAINE 'FIENDS' ARE a NEW SOUTHERN MENACE: Murder and Insanity Increasing Among Lower Class Blacks Because They Have Taken to 'Sniffing' Since Deprived of Whisky by Prohibition." Funny how "cancel culture" never came for this paper, and all it's racist headlines.

Rewriting it we end up with something similar to modern-day headlines in the mainstream media. "ORANGE MENACE: How Increased Insanity by Mentally Unfit President Led to Travel Ban, Targeting Lower Class Muslims, Hispanics, and Blacks for Murder."

The left's disdain has no basis in reality; it is simply an emotional outrage brought about by a politically infiltrated media. They used manufactured narratives and bad acting to convince the audience that orange is evil. They used little facts relying heavily on outrage driven headlines, saying things like "Unbelievable what Donald J Trump did today... gasp.." Of all the outrageous things he has done, which one sticks out the most?

- "Donald Trump's Wrong. Mexicans Aren't Going to Rape You."
- "Trump Didn't Just Banish a Baby. He Banished a Mother"
- "NY Times editor on Trump headline: It was a 'f—ing' mess"
- ~~"Trump Urges Unity vs. Racism"~~ "Assailing Hate But Not Guns"
- "There Will Be Hell Toupee"
- "Trump Supporter Attacks Muslim Women with Babies, Rips Off Their Hijabs"
- "Trump Pretty Much Admits That He Expects Servicemen to Be Rapists"
- "Donald Trump Calls Hillary Clinton 'The Devil'"
- "Trump Slams Voting Rights for Felons, Wants GOP to Court Black Voters"
- "Hillary Surrogate Says Trump's "Schlong" Remark Was Really About Calling Obama a Black Rapist"
- "Marco Rubio Puts His Life in Donald Trump's Tiny Hands'"

Think about the substance of each? There is none. There is only humor for normal people and sadness for anyone who buys into it, because they are the victim of large scale brainwashing.

Misogyny

They label him a misogynist, but women have started more small businesses than ever before. Ivanka Trump helped him create the Women's Global Development and Prosperity (W-GDP) Initiative, the first-ever whole-of-government approach focused on advancing women's full and free participation in the global economy. How could this be the work of a misogynistic man?

The media watches Trump like a hawk, drudging every day for a sensational story. So far there have been no sex scandals. He did not take advantage of any interns. No island flights booked. No hair sniffed. Women are safe. So, the misogynistic narrative failed to live up to the fear-mongering lies of the left.

Islamophobic

There are many wonderful people from all around the world; they work hard and contribute to human society. These are the people we want to live among us. We must not allow adjectives to control us. We can rightfully decide who we want in our country. It is not immoral to choose who you live with. It is like selecting a roommate or spouse.

There are many in the Islamic faith that are wonderful, compassionate people. However, there are those that hate western civilization. They want to kill us because of our liberal ideologies. Freedom is a threat to their theocratic way of life. Some extremists use the Koran to justify slaughtering Christians, Jews, other Muslims, and homosexuals. Although, the history of other religions is full of death and war; it is a thing of the past.

An extreme element exists in the mostly peaceful Islamic faith. We must not lump these people in with everyday Muslims. It is akin to watching a political hack go on a shooting rampage, and wondering if he is a Democrat or Republican, it does not de-legitimize either party. The Sanders supporter who shot Steve Scalise did not change my opinion of Sanders. It only changed my opinion of the shooter. The media tries to do this with Donald Trump saying that he "insights" violence. He does not, and the Muslim faith does not incite violence. There are crazy people under every tent and if we turn over enough rocks, we will find them.

This includes the police. We have corrupt cops, but we must not lump all cops in with them. When we live in a black and blue world we end up with the police being shot in their car for no reason. It would be as if we said all teachers are pedophiles because a teacher slept with a student. These sorts of oversimplifications lead to dangerous stereotypes that hurt people in our community. Every job in the world has good and bad people because people are good and bad. We cannot know which they are until we get to know them.

We need to do a better job of weeding out the crazy in our society, and Islamic communities are doing a better job of weeding out their extremist. However, a person who chants death to an entire civilization has no business leading a country. Good everyday Muslims need to stand up to extremists in their communities, just as BLM needs to stand up against their extremists. Many have turned a blind eye to the mayhem. Peaceful Muslims must help us combat the extremist to reduce overall suffering. Just as the leftest must take a stand against cop murders and rioters.

Islamic societies bring a different set of cultural values that do not respect women's rights. They are on the extreme right-wing. We must respect their freedom to express their religion, but we cannot allow them to control our society. We should allow Muslims to enter our country, but we must be sure they can adhere to our values and support our constitution. If they cannot, then they are a danger to our citizens and we may stop them.

People need to understand that immigration is our choice, and those choices have a major impact on our society. We have a multitude of races and nationalities in our country, which is great, but we must be sure that everyone believes in freedom and the American way. If people are hostile to our way of life and push to open Sharia Courts in our cities, then everything will change.

If there is a threat coming from a certain region based on CIA intelligence, then our Commander-in-Chief has every right to shut down immigration from that region. I would not care if it was Ireland. We should remain cautious. It has nothing to do with religions or skin colors. Not to pause immigration would be a dereliction of duty. A liberal president would hesitate, and another huge attack could jolt our country for many years.

This is the conundrum we face. Ninety-nine percent of all people that enter from these countries are harmless to our country. Perhaps they wouldn't agree with our liberal tendencies, but they would not cause harm. However, if someone laced one candy in a bag with a deadly poison, would you give the bag to your kid hoping they don't eat the wrong one?

It is better to throw the bag of candy away? We do not owe things to people from different countries. They are not citizens of our country. They are not Americans. Most of them do not believe in our Constitution, and therefore, do not deserve its protections. We can be nice to them and keep our doors open to them, but they have to work on eliminating the radical element in their society.

There are extremists in the Islamic community that have no problem killing or being killed to make a point. The point to us being, they hate our freedoms and want us to change. They think killing us will cause it and they are right to an extent, but eventually things will go back to normal. There will be a time when this is a footnote in the history books and we can open up to the wonderful cultures in Arab countries. With Trump's Middle Eastern peace deal hopeful the world will dawn on that time very soon.

Never-Trump Republicans

Nothing irritates me more than weak-minded Republicans who cannot support their causes or candidates. A group so paralyzed by the left that they cannot stand up for what is right. Trump is not one of these kinds of Republicans, therefore he is my kind of Republican.

People like John Kasich who spoke at the Democratic National Convention like a bitter child. He was upset that somebody stole his presidency. It began back in the 2016 Republican primary when he grew very concerned over Trump's comments towards women. He has yet to show the manifestation of those concerns. What has Trump done to women since becoming president? Did he fly off to a private island with a bunch of pedophiles?

The immaturity of John Kasich is astounding. He became so emotional he pushed himself into a liberal corner. Normally after a primary, you give a concession speech and support the candidate. Holding a grudge for three years, then speaking at the opposing party's political convention makes you look like a sore loser. Perhaps he can relate to the bitterness in the Democratic party. A group that is so full of injustices, tribal divisions, and hateful anti-American propaganda. What does it say about his conservative values that he can support a Biden-Sanders platform? That he is not outraged by Bill Clinton's exploits? Now he is a man without a home, as the Democrats will never fully embrace him, but only use him for political fodder against Trump. Then they will dispose of him.

Other establishment types like Jeff Flake claim to be preserving the integrity of the White House. What he means to say is that he wants to keep the elites in power because it was a system he fed off of. He is a corrupt political insider. How can a Republican in good conscience support Joe Biden and his anti-police rhetoric? The answer is he was never a Republican. He was a wolf in sheep's clothing and Trump unmasked him for all the world to see.

Other cowards like Mitt Romney fall into the same political void. So eager for acceptance by the mainstream media that they sell out their principles for admittance. Trump has a way of bringing them to the surface. It is our duty as American citizens to vote them out of office.

Trump has this unique ability to ensnare the Never-Trump political class. By way of example, Senator Marco Rubio unbelievably cowered to the left during a CNN town hall debate on gun control after the Stoneman Douglas High School shooting. He appeared to be a man more driven by polling data than truth. He could have said, this is a right enshrined in our Constitution! A sacred gift from our founding fathers! We must not destroy it.

Other Republicans like John McCain who failed to repeal the disastrous Obamacare because he had a friendship with Obama's legacy. We must always place principles over political allegiances. Sad to see an American Vet trade in his hero card for a seat at the Obama luncheon.

Colin Powell has supported Democrats in every election since he left office. Yet somehow was a Republican? A man who disgraced himself by falsely reporting on Weapons of Mass Destruction at the UN. He lacks bedrock principles. How else could he support an out-of-control liberal agenda?

Last is George W. Bush, who had a ton of political capital after 9/11 and used it for the Patriot Act and the Iraq War. He has never embraced Trump, instead he favors Barack Obama and Ellen DeGeneres. Fitting in my mind because Bush and Obama are a coin toss for the worst president in American history.

Bush led us into an illegitimate, worthless war, and Obama spied on the opposing party without probable cause. A crime reminiscent of Watergate except for its lack of media coverage. Contrasted by the audacity of Obama to use the FBI instead of Nixon, who hired 5 random guys. Our media did not cover the story because Obama was a "legendary candidate of historical significance," and to speak poorly of him was racist.

In Conclusion

Trump has many personality flaws, as we all do, but none of them disqualify him from the presidency. I do not want a saint leading my country, because no one living in this much sunlight is a saint. It would only be a disguise. People in disguise are dangerous and hard to figure out.

Love him or hate him, Trump has produced results (y). This is quite a feat, considering the defiant opposition, and it should be what we judge him on. Under his presidency, millions of new jobs were created, taxes were cut, regulations were cut, conservative judges appointed, the stock market peaked, the individual mandate of ObamaCare was repealed, border security was tightened, ISIS was pushed back, trade deficits tackled, military power was strengthened, North Korean dialogue initiated, Historic Middle Eastern Peace Agreements and so on.

On the international stage, Trump stopped sending airplanes full of cash to Iran. The Obama theory was that it would deter the development of a nuclear weapon. The reality is that the money was probably used to carry out coordinated attacks against US troops in Iraq by people like General Qasem Soleimani who Trump righteously killed at the Baghdad Airport. Why is an Iranian general in Iraq? Iran, the country we are paying to be our friend. The country that is the number one state sponsor of terror in the world. Withdrawing from the horrible, one-sided Iran Deal was a great move.

Trump moved the U.S. Embassy to Jerusalem and brokered a historic peace deal in the Middle East. Israel and the United Arab Emirates agreed to Advance Peace and Prosperity in the Region. A major step to a less war-prone middle east. This was done by him siding strongly with Israel and sending the message that nobody was going to push them into the sea. People tend to back down when they know they will not win. With Obama, they felt like they had a chance to obliterate Israel.

Much like Israel, we need to be protected from people that do not share our values and want to kill us. Using things like a travel ban against people who wish to harm us is pragmatic. Why take unnecessary risks? It seems with the virus going around, most people are OK with limited travel. However, when it was terrorists going around, people wanted to play politics. We want to be open to the world, but the world has to mature in certain places. Nobody would open their blue doors up in a neighborhood full of violent felons who openly target blue doors.

Beyond all the bickering, most rational people agree with his platform. He deserves credit for trying to accomplish everything he talked about on the campaign trail. Accomplishments achieved despite being hamstrung by Never-Trump Republicans, Deep-State Swamp Rats, Democrats, the Muller Investigation, Fake News Outlets, left-wing mobs, BLM, Antifa, and Hollywood elites. It has been an entertaining battle.

Trump has not failed the American people, we have failed him. We took away the House of Representatives, gave ratings to the leftist lies on TV, played weak bi-partisan games with the Muller Investigation, hired feckless mayors that allowed angry mobs to burn our city streets, took irrational measures to stop the virus, and gave millions to Marxist organizations like BLM. Our poor collective decision making has led to a less prosperous nation.

Trump stands strong, fighting it all off. He does not cower to the left or attempt to please their obnoxious feelings. Trump is real. He speaks his mind. Perhaps you dislike his mind, but at least you know it. He does not hide behind an army of political polishers. He takes the time to hear different sides before deciding. He is a man who has the courage of his convictions and has enjoyed my support since the escalator.

10 Reasons for Trump

1. Great Leader

The more you listen to Trump, the more you realize he is not the orange villain others portray him to be. He is not an ideologue or partisan hack. While in business he donated, complemented, and associated with politicians of all sides. He is an open-minded moderate, who welcomes opposing voices, and has a good sense of humor.

2. Keeps his Promises

He has clearly defined goals and stays on target. The things he could not accomplish are the fault of his opposition. He is not a king; he cannot fire Nancy Pelosi.

3. Better Platform

The economy thrives under lower taxes and reduced regulation. His unemployment numbers were some of the lowest in history and his GDP growth numbers were impressive. He has worked towards making America energy independent by supporting fracking, coal mining, and pipelines. His agenda has a far greater output (y) than that of the liberals.

4. Transparency

Trump openly communicates with the American people. We know his stance on every major issues. This openness is a breath of fresh air. Transparency is rare in Washington and we should welcome it. People seem offended by him being a real person.

5. Immigration

We admit about 1.1 million people per year into the United States legally. The line is millions deep and we have an obligation to our future generations to ensure that those coming here respect our values, especially freedom. We should implement a merit-based immigration policy, not a racist quota-driven policy that considers skin color.

6. Pandemic Reaction

The left tries to paint his reaction to the virus as a flaw when it is a great strength. The virus put us all in an impossible situation and he maintained his cool. He did not panic, nor did he push Americans into a panic. This could have been so much worse if he was a power-hungry authoritarian. He could have subdued the entire nation; something Hillary Clinton would have done. Trump acted quickly and decisively to block travel but did not overreact with lockdowns, leaving it up to the states. In Democrat-run states, they have dramatically overreacted to the virus. They have created panic either hoping to hurt Trump or because they are natural authoritarians. Biden has flirted with the idea of shutting down the entire nation and forcing everyone to wear a mask.

7. Fights the Left

The radical left has gone too far with their fake news, cancel culture, and socialist agenda. We must stop them. Trump stands up for free speech. The radical left has taken over the Democratic Party. Far out ideas like the Green New Deal will be front and center in the Biden administration. Biden lacks the strength to stand up to AOC and her squad.

8. Independent of Special Interest

He is not beholden to special interest; this frees him up to make decisions that are in the best interest of all Americans. No one can control his Twitter habit, not his own family, or even his own fingers. He bleeds transparency. He is a true patriot. He is not owned by any shadowy figures. Only a partisan hack would believe that a foreign actor could control him. He listens to everyone but takes orders from no one. He has American interest at heart and we are Americans.

9. Judicial Nominations

He has appointed a record number of conservatives to the bench and will have a chance at one more Supreme Court justice.

10. Liberals Hate Him

They hate Trump like a toddler that hates going to bed early. Sitting high atop their Twitter perches, they rain down on the sitting President of the United States, ironically labeling him a narcissist.

4

Harris on the Ticket

Who is Kamala Harris?

With "Sleepy Joe" safely tucked away in the basement, we shift our focus to Kamala Harris. She is the daughter of a Jamaican-born Stanford professor and an Indian medical researcher. Born after the Civil Rights bill of 1964, she grew up in the liberal bastions of California and Canada, yet claims to be oppressed. She often speaks of her struggles growing up black, only mentioning her Indian heritage when it suits her. In the humanistic world of identity politics, the black card Trumps the Indian card and she plays it cunningly. Without her color, she would not have qualified for the vice-presidential nomination as it was a declared prerequisite.

An unpopular opinion: Using someone's skin color should not play a part in their selection, whether it is positive or negative - that is the very definition of discrimination. But this is expected from a party that was formerly racist against the black community and is now "justifiably" racist against white people. There is no legitimate reason for such a prerequisite. Civil Rights leaders of the past would be rolling over in their graves due to this injustice. Modern Democrats lack the foundational morals to stand for what is right, only doing what is politically expedient. They rejoice over Harris' historical diversity in their headlines, discarding the fact that she lacks the basic integrity necessary to be Vice President.

In the Democratic primary, as her campaign gained momentum, her poll numbers plummeted. This ruptured her deep lust for power, causing her to lash out and accuse the Democratic party of not being "woke" enough to nominate a woman of color. A party that chooses a black man and a white woman was not ready for them simultaneously. In her opinion, it had nothing to do with her obvious flip-flops designed to placate an irrational mob. This illuminates her egotistical view of reality and her self-serving bias. When she is not in power, she will condemn others for not supporting her rather than acknowledging her own unworthiness of their support. Humility does not exist in this woman.

During a powder puff interview with Samantha Bee, she argued that the virus resources should be handed out based on race. "The disparities that have long existed based on race are now highlighted," Kamala Harris said. "So one of the things that I'm calling for around this pandemic is that we make decisions about where the resources should go based on that issue." This is a sick and twisted take on affirmative action. Perhaps she thinks that allowing white people to die in the back of the vaccine line because of historical injustices will quell racial division. This is an endeavor to gain political favor with the black community by using divisive politics. If she wants to make an argument to discriminate, it should be based on age and not race.

It is akin to creating a lunch line and allowing certain ethnic groups to eat first while others have to wait in the back. Except instead of food, it is life-saving resources - this creates resentment, which leads to an increase in racism. Blacks vote overwhelmingly for the Democratic Party which is why she loves them so much, not because she identifies with them. She uses them as a tool to fulfill her power agenda. She plays them with the race card and watches the results pour in like winning a jackpot of stupidity.

When she accepted the powerful Vice Presidential nomination, there was a genuine joy in her voice. It was her big payday for being a diverse candidate willing to appease an angry mob and suck up to tech giants, for those countless hours of listening to her handlers and doing everything they say. Her eagerness can be overwhelming at times. She was chosen so that she can be controlled through her ambition. She will say and do anything to remain in power.

In San Francisco, at the age of 29, her political career began by sleeping with a 60-year-old married mayor named Willie Brown. He then appointed her to the California Unemployment Insurance Appeals Board and later to the Medical Assistance Commission. What does this say about a person? Using identity to advance a political career is one thing but using sexuality is an entirely different ballgame.

She has no kids, so she lives off the rush of rising power. She speaks of regulating what we eat and how we drink. She wants to control our speech, guns, straws, hamburgers, and cars. These kinds of overbearing politicians will ruin the United States. They have already ruined one of our most beautiful states - California. They have turned it into an overtaxed bureaucratic nightmare that lacks fundamental freedom. Hundreds of thousands flee from their output each year.

Harris wants to unlock the gates and let in as many people as possible. Why? Because immigrants overwhelmingly vote for the Democratic Party. They are the key to her irrational victory over the so-called evil white Republicans. How can she be for open borders and free Medicare for all, even illegal immigrants? These two ideas combined will bankrupt our nation. People will flood our country and the medical bills alone would cost us over 3.4 trillion dollars per 330 million people per year.

Bear in mind our allotted discretionary spending for 2020 was only 1.4 trillion dollars! Tripling it would put everyone under extraordinary tax burdens. However, she claims to be able to do it without raising taxes on the middle-class. An obvious lie designed to fool ignorant voters. The liberal base only knows feelings and the liberal elites only know power. It is like a high school student promising free beer at lunch to become president of the student body. It sounds good and riles up the mob, but there is no practical implementation, no way to get it passed by the principal or teachers.

If a poll stated that 16-year-old teenagers would overwhelmingly vote Democratic, then she would be in favor of it. When asked about it in a town hall, she said that the more people are involved in the electoral process, the more "robust" it would be. The reason they want to mail out ballots to millions of Americans is that it will lead to more votes and improve their odds of victory. That or it will murky the waters so bad they could appoint Biden. If any common-sense measures are put in place to ensure a valid election process, they scream voter suppression. In a country where one cannot buy liquor without an ID, one should not be allowed to vote in an election without it.

Teenagers are an impressionable group who can be easily lured into the trappings of socialism. The focus is on the input of helping mankind and ignoring the output of social destruction. They do not yet have the mental acuity to completely understand the bigger picture. They become entangled in a bitter web spun by the liberals, unable to free themselves.

The people we live near heavily influence our politics. The interest of the independent farmer would never be heard if it were not for the Electoral College. Democrats dominate our populated cities and therefore could easily dominate most of our elections. It is mind-boggling to see a political map and notice how much influence people have over each other in terms of politics. Neighbors and family all influencing each other. Our founding fathers had the wisdom to understand our propensity for groupthink. Thus, they created an electoral college to insure the rights of all people were represented.

Our forefathers had the intelligence to know that power had to be spread out, and therefore they created the Electoral College. The Democrats detest it because it costs them power. They still complain about Hillary Clinton losing the election despite winning the popular vote. She knows the rules of our democracy and should have valiantly accepted the results of the election.

Anything that stands in the left's way must be crushed. For instance, when Tulsi Gabbard dropped some truth bombs on Harris at a primary debate, it knocked Harris' campaign off the rails but put Gabbard under the boot of the elites. They accused her of being a Russian asset. As ludicrous as it sounded coming from Hillary Clinton's mouth, it was a Democratic laser designator designed to take Gabbard out. Considering Clinton is a former first lady, secretary of state, and senator, one might assume she would have the inside knowledge before making such an outrageous assertion. It was a powerful smear that dismantled Gabbard's campaign. Since then she has sued Clinton for it.

Why was the Democratic machine so furious with one of their own, a former military hero that served in Iraq? Because Gabbard pointed out Harris' terrible track record as an attorney general and DA in California. Harris was not a champion for the oppressed. She kept a man on death row, denying his request for DNA testing. Evidence that can exonerate him as he is still trapped on death row. Standing between Harris and her ambition is a dangerous thing. The death row inmate's name is Kevin Cooper. The case is still swirling around the California justice system as if they are unable to test DNA. They understand the danger it possesses to Kamala Harris' reputation, which is infinitely more important than a potentially innocent man's life. If he must rot in jail or be executed, it is acceptable collateral damage. Although, she has always been "personally" opposed to the death penalty because it tracked better in the focus groups. Her public stance on this controversial topic is unreliable.

She once fought a judge's ruling that labeled the death penalty as unconstitutional. Yet, two days after police officer Renata Espinoza was gunned down by a gang member using an AK-47 in San Francisco, DA Harris went on TV to declare she would not seek the death penalty. This greatly upset the family, a family she did not console or consult and outraged the community. She refused to respond to a letter that the slain police officer's wife wrote to her. It is disappointing that in such a high profile case, Harris would not do the right thing and reach out to the family. After describing herself as the "top cop" one might assume she would show a little bit of empathy for a devastated police officer's family. To this day, she refuses to answer why she didn't personally reach out to the family, only briefly meeting with them once in jest.

The 'new' Harris is 'woke' and soft on crime unlike her tenure as Attorney General when she locked up a 29-year-old reality TV star and aspiring hip-hop artist, Jamal Trulove. He was convicted of murdering Seu Kuka based on one woman's testimony who was paid by the prosecution. He was allegedly set up by the cops and it was overturned on appeals because the case had been mishandled by Harris' office. He was awarded millions of dollars and set free. There was no justice for the taxpayers.

The new version of slavery is not cotton and plantations, it is drugs and prisons. Years ago, she hurt minorities by putting them in jail beyond their prison terms, probably exploiting them for cheap labor. Fitting for someone whose grandparents owned 125 slaves in Jamaica. Who is she? Does she have a principal to stand up against racism? Is she a victim of racism? Or a creature of the swamp, adapting to the most advantageous form to fit in her environment. She put over 1,500 people in jail for marijuana, then laughed about smoking pot on a radio show. During that interview, she seemed like an unpopular kid trying to fit in. Is that the real her or is she the poor little innocent schoolgirl that accused Joe Biden of being a segregationist?

During the Democratic primary debate, she honed in on Biden working with racists to oppose forced busing. She insinuated that he was a racist, which could have some merit. Forced busing was a tool used to diversify communities. The idea was that segregated schools put black people at an academic disadvantage. It ignored the importance of the family in one's development and it did not help us unify as both white and black parents opposed it. Moving children across large cities every day was taxing. Engagement in after school activities declined as well as parental attendance. Schools are the pillars of our communities - moving everything around only succeeded in ruining the education system. It is a typical liberal idea. Divide people based on skin color then force them into a diverse mix to satisfy racial quotas. This does nothing but make people feel like colored dots on an academic paper.

There is no person Harris will not slander for political gain. Going after her running mate on grounds of racial discrimination and sexual misconduct is foul. She said, referring to four of Joe Biden's accusers, "I believe them." Destroying a white man's reputation is nothing new for her. She also went after Brett Kavanagh, which was absurd.

Our history is well acquainted with extremely ambitious individuals. They are a dangerous reminder of the well-intended evils that we, as humans, face. The damage they can inflict with their noble missions in the name of "social justice" is unimaginable. They are overconfident in their ability to fix flaws, but in reality, they will turn our nation into smoldering ash. It is not her fault for being who she is; the blame lies with California for being what it is. How could a state of seemingly intelligent people produce such a vile candidate to represent them nationally?

She was elevated not based on her merit but based on white guilt. They just read the historically diverse headlines and never bothered to dig into the fine print. In the national spotlight, we get a clearer picture. An overly ambitious racist who wants to carve up the Constitution. Locking people up for expressing freedom is detrimental to our society. People like Harris have this odd desire to try and control us. If she had her way, people would be spending time in jail for using plastic straws and saying 'China Virus'. Free speech should be a red-line for all of us. There is no justifiable explanation for taking away freedom of speech. We are Americans.

Harris went as far as to introduce a bill (116th Cong., 2nd session S. Res 580) that would put serious limitations on free speech. The bill would ban all forms of what it termed derogatory speech. Phrases such as "Chinese Virus," "Wuhan Virus," and "King Flu" would be classified as racist and therefore banned, ignoring the unanimous Supreme Court verdict protecting speech in America as well as the first amendment to the constitution.

What is her agenda? How could she ever hope to enact this legislation? Perhaps, after attracting immigrants from around the world with free healthcare, welfare, education, and open borders, she could flood the country with enough votes to amend the Constitution. Flushing 243 years of wisdom down the drain, for a bitter liberal from California. The disturbing part is the bill was supported by 25 Senate Democrats, including Elizabeth Warren, Amy Klobuchar and Bernie Sanders.

Destroying people's rights in this manner creates a toxic environment and escalates problems. Problems for which she claims to be the solution. Ironically, her absence is the actual solution so we must vote her off the political stage. So we must vote her off the political stage. We do not need politicians baiting people into rioting, saying incendiary op-ed rhetoric like, "The time for outrage is now. The time for solidarity is now. The time for action is now. The time for change is now," when we need calm minds to unify.

Nobody wants to live under an overbearing authoritarian. Harris said that she would pass the Green New Deal by eliminating the filibuster, also known as the nuclear option. She would push half the country into submission based on her radical ideology. It could tear us apart economically and racially. Not to mention the reparation clauses trying to force whites who did not own slaves to pay back blacks who were not slaves is wrong. A new form of genetic crime would have to be created. Perhaps we should lock up Jeffery Dahmer's sister for being his relative.

She pushes these extreme positions because she knows it covers up her past. Even Joe Biden noted in the primary that she oversaw a forensic lab that distorted over 1,000 cases. While she has denied knowledge of the problematic lab when it was discovered, she failed to inform the defense lawyers. A judge ruled that she broke the law by failing to inform the defendants. 1,000 cases had to be overturned because of her. Others said she was made aware yet pushed through the convictions anyway.

This is backed up by her statements that there should be serious and severe consequences to crime. She lives in fear because she has been in the courtroom with the nastiest people of society. She said she had three locks on her door, yet now she wants to reduce the number of police and jails. She fought for cash bail, which unjustly punishes poor people. A woman that once stood for swift and severe punishment now wants social justice reform? What changed besides the polls? Or is that all that matters?

If ever elected or appointed president, she said she would regulate firearms with an executive action. Imagine losing your right to bear arms over an unconstitutional executive action. Reminds me of the New York lawyers attacking the NRA. Why are these new Democrats so hostile to our right to bear arms? Have they forgotten the lessons of history? That a population with limited speech and no arms is easily controlled and helpless to stop it! Oh wait, that is their end goal! Control over everything! It's nothing new. Our history is littered with ambitious politicians lusting for power.

She wants to start with mandatory gun buybacks for AR-15's. Although less than 1% of all gun deaths are committed by this type of rifle. She wants to disarm people that do not vote for her. In other words, she wants to use armed defunded tax-subsidized police officers to force tax-paying armed citizens to give up their right to bear arms, while she keeps her taxpayer-funded armed security detail. Who is this woman?

Is Kamala Harris the "pragmatic moderate" the media portrays her to be or is she the most liberal senator in America? According to govtrack.us, a non-partisan group, based on her voting record, she is the most liberal senator in America, even more liberal than Bernie Sanders and Elizabeth Warren. According to the New York Times ginned up opinion piece, she is a pragmatic moderate. Unless you went back to the November 29, 2019 article about her campaign unraveling. How does one paper have two wildly contrasting views of the same person? Because they have only one mission, to defeat Donald Trump and their opinions can be contoured into any position to achieve it.

What makes her so liberal?

- She voted against bipartisan legislation more than any other senator
- She threatened executive action to confiscate guns
- She kind of supports Medicare for All
- She supported eliminating private insurance until she didn't
- She supports open borders and welfare increases
- She called for outrage on our city streets, egging on riots
- Original co-sponsor of the radical Green New Deal
- She wrote a bill that would limit free speech
- She used to incarcerate marijuana users, now she admits to smoking it
- She compared law enforcement to the KKK
- Is against the death penalty yet appealed a judge's decision to stop executions
- She wants to eliminate private prisons and mandatory sentences
- Called for the virus aid to be handed out disproportionately, based on race
- She is wildly pro-abortion including taxpayer abortion on demand
- Against fracking and coal

While in the Senate, she voted against a bipartisan piece of legislation that would provide a path to citizenship for dreamers and fund the wall. Time and time again, she has proven that she has no desire to reach across the aisle. She would be a divisive leader, ruling with a phone and a pen, hammering her progressive agenda down on half our nation. Our only hope would be the Supreme Court censoring her power, as the feeble Congress will be stuck in gridlock.

She was rebuked by the Senate for questioning a judicial nominees' religious affiliation. Brian Buescher, a Catholic man, was nominated for the US District Court of Nebraska. Anti-Catholicism is something one of our great presidents John F. Kennedy had to face. She ignored Article VI Section 3 of the Constitution which clearly states that, "No religious Test shall ever be required as a Qualification to any Office or public Trust under the United States." She violated the constitution knowingly and for political gain. She is disqualified for higher office in my opinion.

The landmark Civil Rights Proposition 209 in California bars race, ethnicity, or gender preferences when hiring, considering admission to a college, or taking government actions. Kamala Harris sent a letter to the Supreme Court to undercut it. She wants to allow universities the right to consider race in admissions. She wants to discriminate against Asians and whites, punishing them for scoring disproportionately high on their ACT & SAT tests.

Why does she want to lead a nation that she is so hostile towards? She has no respect for our history, our constitution, or the color blind tone of our Civil Rights movement. She is a new breed of Democrat, one sent to tear down white male America, antagonistic to anyone who votes Republican. She has built up agitation towards the first amendment, specifically free speech and freedom of religion. She thinks limiting or abolishing the second amendment will somehow cure the ills of society. She wants reparations to be paid to slave descendants, but she has no plan for implementation.

Unknowingly she is a Trojan horse for a radical path that will destroy our nation. All these well-intended things will only divide us further and push our nation to the brink of civil war. A nasty virus named socialism has infiltrated the Democratic Party, and they are either too weak to defeat it or too myopic on defeating Trump to effectively deal with it.

In summary, Kamala Harris said that she believed the four women who accused Joe Biden of inappropriate touching, and in a debate, she inferred he was a racist. The unanswered questions now are: Is Joe Biden a racist white male sexual predator? And if so, why does she want to be his Vice President? And if not, why would she lie and falsely accuse him?

Perhaps because power means more to her than principles. If she truly believed he was a predator, then she should have rejected his offer. If she does not believe that he is a predator, then she should have never said it. She cannot have it both ways. Either he is a predator and she opposes it or he is not, and she falsely accused him. Why? For political expediency, thinking it would catapult her in front of him. She would tarnish a good man's record for political power and accept a terrible man's offer for political power. How can anyone support this transparent lack of integrity? Millions of Americans are blinded by the media's glowing diversity praise.

Ten Final Questions for Kamala

How can we accept a person as Vice President who refuses to answer basic questions about her past? Would we accept a person's job application if they refused to answer any questions? This is the 2nd most important job in the world, and if she cannot answer a few straightforward questions she does not deserve it. This is completely unacceptable in a free democracy. If reporters won't ask them then Mike Pence needs to stop the debate and ask them.

- Is Joe Biden a sexual predator or did you rush to judgment and falsely accuse an innocent man?
- What does this say about your judgment as an ex-DA/AG?
- Do you condemn the Portland group of BLM protesters who openly rejoiced in the cold-blooded murder of a Trump supporter?
- Will you condemn Antifa and BLM by name for rioting in Portland and trying to burn down a courthouse?
- Why do you support never ending protest?
- Hate speech or freedom of speech?
- Should the virus aid be handed out disproportionately based on race?
- Financially, how can you have open borders and free healthcare for immigrants without raising taxes on the middle-class?
- When are you going to reply to Officer Espinoza's wife's letter?
- Is Jussie Smollett innocent, Brett Kavanaugh guilty and the Russia hoax true?

5

Questions about Joe Biden

Who is Joe Biden?

C'mon man! Why did Joe Biden make such a bad VP pick? Did he even make it? Questions we may never know the answer to because Joe Biden does not answer questions. For his base, this is acceptable because he is NOT TRUMP. This is his most redeeming quality. However, because he wants to run our country we should know a little more about him. Who is Joe Biden?

He was born in 1942 in Scranton, Pennsylvania, to a mother and father of Irish, English, and French descent. His father worked in the oil industry and as a used car salesman. Joe grew up with a stutter, something he valiantly overcame. His academics were poor but he was popular playing athletics and being elected class president. He was unable to fight in Vietnam due to asthma. After graduating from the University of Delaware in 1965, he met and married Neilia Hunter. Later he graduated from Syracuse Law School and lied about finishing in the top half of his class. One of many lies he would tell throughout his political career.

Biden's wife and daughter were tragically killed in an automobile accident in 1972. The next year he would run for the Delaware Senate seat. A post he served from 1973 to 2009. On the outside, he seems like a politician willing to reach across the aisle and make deals, more so than Kamala.

During his long tenure in the Senate, most of his legislative focus was on crime. Liberals constantly speak of "justice reform" and "oppressive systems" but what they do not realize is that they are trying to change a system that Joe Biden more than anyone else helped create. In his own words on the Senate floor, Biden said, "The truth is, every major crime bill since 1976 that's come out of this Congress, every minor crime bill, has had the name of the Democratic senator from the State of Delaware: Joe Biden."

This justice system unfairly disadvantages minorities by having laws that give vastly different sentences for similar crimes, things like powder cocaine vs crack cocaine. Biden helped write and pass the 1986 law that made the punishment for crack cocaine (used by low-income minorities) more severe than powder cocaine (used by white elites). He helped usher in a new era of the war on drugs, which incarcerated countless minorities. Millions serving half their lives for petty crimes on "gateway" drugs like Marijuana.

He did it by passing countless bills that people on the left would abhor if they ever knew about, but are unaware of it because the media fails to report on it. Our media has turned into a political machine hell-bent on destroying Trump. Ignoring all the times Biden met with the Chinese. He sought to have his Senate records sealed by the University of Delaware. We may never know what they discussed. But where are Trump's taxes? That's all that matters.

Biden is a creature of the swamp, a Washington political insider willing to sacrifice anything for power. He has a long history full of racist gaffes and terrible legislation. The Democrats should have chosen a more vibrant candidate, someone like Tulsa Gabbard, but they refused because she cannot be easily controlled. They can however control Joe Biden. They forced his VP pick and pushed him to aligned his platform with Bernie Sanders.

Is Joe Biden a Racist?

Joe Biden's record must be ignored, or it would be his undoing. The most disqualifying thing is revealed by an old adage: people oftentimes accuse others of what they are guilty of themselves. Biden and the Democrats, without any evidence, convinced half our nation that Donald Trump is a racist. Perhaps Joe Biden is the real racist.

We begin with segregation, or specifically busing—an idea that Joe Biden considered "bankrupt." Busing was an attempt to manually desegregate black and white schools. The idea was; after civil rights legislation, the nation needed to be pushed to ensure all schools complied with the new integration laws. The vision was black and white students co-mingling.

Modern Democrats do not agree, people like Kamala Harris called Biden out in the primary debates for working with racist senators on bussing legislation. She prefaced her remarks by saying she did not believe he was a racist but attributed racist characteristics to him. It highlights an interesting point; Is Joe Biden a racist? Can a racist change over time? If racists are redeemable, why is our nation not? Why doesn't the "cancel culture" come for Joe Biden?

Associates

Biden worked closely with Senator Strom Thurmond, who was a racist segregationist, in order to oppose bussing. Thurman was a Democrat, who vehemently opposed the civil rights act of 1964. Joe Biden eulogized him in 2003 by saying, "The truth and genius and virtue of Strom Thurmond is what I choose and we all choose to remember today." Biden said Thurmond was one of his closest friends.

How could Joe Biden praise a white racist from South Carolina? This is probably what Kamala Harris was talking about in the primary debates when she said, "It was hurtful to hear you talk about the reputations of two United States senators who built their reputations and career on the segregation of race in this country."

Almost all Americans alive today see the civil rights act of 1964 as the key piece of legislation that ended government-sanctioned racism in our nation. Thurmond was a die-hard segregationist who said, "I want to tell you, ladies and gentlemen, that there's not enough troops in the army to force the Southern people to break down segregation and admit the N**** race into our theaters, into our swimming pools, into our homes, and into our churches." He embodied the reason black people could not drink out of the same water fountains as whites. He staged the longest filibuster in American history, speaking for 24 hours and 18 minutes against the 1957 Civil Rights Act. A bill that ultimately failed.

Biden also had kind words for Democratic Alabama Governor George Wallace, whom many consider being the most racist politicians of the modern era. Biden said of the late governor, "I think the Democratic Party could stand a liberal George Wallace - Someone who's not afraid to stand up and offend people, someone who wouldn't pander but would say what the American people know in their gut is right."

Wallace claimed to have lost the Alabama governor's race in 1958 by being in his words "out n****ed." Wallace won the 1962 race by embracing the KKK. He stood in the doorway of the University of Alabama in 1963 to try and keep black college students from enrolling. He also tried to prevent four black elementary students from going to a predominantly white school in Huntsville, Alabama. He used the infamous "Segregation now, segregation forever!" rallying cry to stir up his racist white base.

Wallace also supported a pit-bull like a cop named Theophilus "Bull" Connor, who violently opposed the civil rights protesters. Bull Connor was a Democrat and the Commissioner of Public Safety for Birmingham, overseeing the Fire and Police department for more than 20 years. He denied civil rights to blacks and enforced racial segregation. He outraged the entire nation with some of his horrendous actions, which ultimately catalyzed the passing of the 1964 civil rights legislation. Under his reign, the black community suffered a massive number of casualties and abuses. Over 100 black people were killed in Jefferson County in Alabama, during the 1932 to 1968 civil rights movement. Dogs and fire hydrants were used to torture people. It was one of the most racist police departments in the world.

Beyond being a racist Wallace was a terrible human being. He used his wife to bypass the gubernatorial term limit rule. When he found out she had cancer halfway through the campaign he hid it from her so she would keep campaigning. She died soon after partly because she never received treatment. Do we need more like him? A man that would embrace the KKK and let his wife die of cancer for political power? What does this say about Joe Biden's judgment?

In 2008 during his VP campaign in Charleston, West Virginia, Biden was photographed with Robert Byrd. Byrd was a former chapter leader of the KKK, and infamously filibustered the civil rights act of 1964 by speaking on the Senate floor for 14 hours. In 2010 Biden called Byrd a mentor, guide, and friend.

He called another racist senator John Stennis (D-MS) a man of character. Stennis opposed Brown Versus the Board of Education, wanting to replace it with a deeply racist system called the Southern Manifesto. In addition, Biden said of three segregationist senators: Herman Talmadge, Jesse Helms, and James Eastland, "All of these men became my friends."

If one prefers to see things in writing Joe Biden sent letters to Eastland, who was a racist plantation owner, thanking him for helping in the fight against busing. Biden said, "I want you to know that I very much appreciate your help during this week's Committee meeting in attempting to bring my anti-busing legislation to a vote,"

Joe Biden is a relic from the past whose lone "diversity credential" comes from Barack Obama, a man who would not openly endorse him until after the primary. Obama's speeches tend to focus more on Donald Trump than Joe Biden. Why? Because Obama used Biden as a racist prop to ensure the support of industrial white Americans. Joe Biden for VP was a political calculation by Obama designed to racially balance himself out, thinking that America was not ready for two minorities on a ticket.

Biden once made the slightly racist comment about Obama, "I mean you got the first mainstream African-American who is articulate and bright and clean and a nice-looking guy- I mean, that's a storybook, man." One time a frustrated Obama said privately, "How many times is he going to say something stupid?" Calling them "Joe Bombs" But fortunately for Obama, Biden was invisible during the campaign.

The media always exclaims how 'presidential' Obama is, ignoring all the partisan things he does. He gave a campaign speech during a funeral. The memorial service of John Lewis is not the place to attack Trump, it is a time for morning and unity. Not only was it disrespectful to the family but also the nation. There is a time and place for everything and Obama nor Biden seem to understand that. One time as VP Biden talked about the hypothetical assassination of Obama at a town hall event dedicated to healthcare.

Legislation

More important than his racist associates was the legislation that he helped pass. Joe Biden criticized Republican presidents Ronald Reagan and George HW Bush for not being tough enough on drugs and crime. As mentioned, he supported or authored almost every major crime bill in his 36-year Senate career. Legislation that destroyed underprivileged communities and disenfranchised blacks. He ravaged them with harsh penalties and massive prison sentences.

The war on drugs is destructive because it creates a broken justice system that disproportionately affects poor communities. Their youth are looking for a way out, and the harder we clamp down on drugs the higher the profit margins become. At a certain point, it becomes entrapment. Imagine not being able to eat for days, then someone offers you $10,000 to make a delivery. Capitalistic instincts would take over and things would get done.

Taking away the freedom to make mistakes is unforgivable, and we must stop it. It is not about gateway drugs or law and order; this is about the right to make mistakes within a home. Drinking alcohol and using crack cocaine are mistakes. We must all allow each other the right to make mistakes; the consequences are too detrimental if we do not. We can end this entire network of criminals and cartels by implementing simple laws that create farms and dispensaries.

The Biden-Thurmond Crime bill of 1982 unsuccessfully sought to create a Drug Czar and increase the use of civil forfeiture, where the police would seize property for auction. It also sought to increase penalties for drug offenses, it reduced bail, created a sentencing commission, and eradicated federal parole. He proposed tons of anti-drug legislation, so much so that the ACLU has repeatedly criticized him. He wanted to shut down big RAVE parties, accusing them of being drug havens.

He reached a compromise with the Reagan administration and helped push through the Comprehensive Crime Control Act of 1984. Later he would go on to support the anti-drug abuse acts of 1986 and 1988. Behind the scenes, he has pushed the most racist anti-freedom pieces of legislation in US history.

He helped author the 1994 Violent Crime Control and Law Enforcement Act, also known as the Crime Bill or self denoted—Biden Bill. It increased the number of police, built more prisons, increased prison sentences, banned assault weapons, and created a federal death penalty, which he was in favor of until he was not. The bill introduced three strikes and eliminated higher education for inmates. As a result, incarceration rates soared from approximately 1.2 million to 2.5 million in the following years. He wanted longer sentences and more legislation. He spoke of marijuana as a gateway drug as recently as 2010 and wanted to heavily punish users.

Beyond our borders, he said that America has a moral duty to involve itself in other countries' matters. In 1998 Biden called for the ouster of Saddam Hussein by military force. Years later he openly supported and voted for the disastrous 2003 war in Iraq. Now he lies, claiming George W. Bush tricked him into the second war saying, "It was a mistake to trust that they weren't going to go to war," said Biden. "They said they were not going to go to war. They said they were just going to get inspectors in. The world, in fact, voted to get inspectors in, and they still went to war." Everybody knew the Bush administration wanted war with Iraq and without Joe Biden's voice in the Senate, they could not have had it.

He encouraged Obama's troop deployments around the world. In Afghanistan, Iraq, Syria, Libya, Yemen, Somalia, and Pakistan. As a Washington insider, he will probably give in to the military-industrial complex, and start a new war in Syria. We do not need to involve ourselves in that country. Trump understands that and has begun withdrawing us from the Middle East.

Biden does not. He said that Trump's withdrawal from Syria is a "complete failure," because it abandons our "Kurdish Partners." We have no business taking sides and propping up governments around the world. It creates instability, cost lives, and money. Biden's election could lead to a war in Syria, which will drag our country back into a failed Middle East policy, undoing everything Trump has done for peace.

Biden flip-flopped on gays in the military. Initially voting to ban homosexuals from service. He voted in favor of the defense of marriage act, which prevented same-sex marriages. Where is the LGBTQ outrage?

Biden has been all over the map with abortion. First, he voted for a bill that would overturn Roe v Wade and let the states decide on the legality of abortion. However, now he is pro-choice. Previously, he was opposed to a pro-abortion litmus test for judges and funding abortions in other countries, now he is not. He supported the Hyde amendment to band federally funded abortions, now he supports repealing all Pro-Life laws including the Hyde Amendment.

At the age of 77, he has flip-flopped enough times to prove he can sell-out his core belief system for political gain. He released a 110-page joint compromise with Bernie Sanders and Alexandria Ocasio-Cortez called the Unity Task Force. Their main focus was on criminal justice reform, climate change, immigration policies, healthcare, and education. As you can imagine the criminal justice reform is an attempt at undoing everything Biden did. Climate change embraces The Green New Deal and healthcare is a push for single-payer. To fund it all would require massive tax increases. Placing huge burdens on the wealthy and middle-class.

Biden has changed his stance so often he should be called Joe Shapeshifter. Will Biden stay true to this flip? Or will he flop again once in power? He voted for welfare cuts, but now he is in favor of increasing welfare spending. Bernie Sanders called him out for flip-flopping on entitlements, Social Security and Medicare. First being in favor of cuts, then changing his mind. He purposefully lied to Bernie's face over and over again. Everything could just be a temporary truce to appease his liberal base and sure up their support in November. Once in power, he will surely do what pleases him, as he mentioned not seeking a 2nd term at the age of 82. Is it possible to teach an old dog new tricks?

Can we trust a man who said in his promotion of the 1994 crime bill, "We have predators on our streets that society has in fact, in part because of its neglect, created...they are beyond the pale many of those people, beyond the pale. And it's a sad commentary on society. We have no choice but to take them out of society....a cadre of young people, tens of thousands of them, born out of wedlock, without parents, without supervision, without any structure, without any conscience developing because they literally ... because they literally have not been socialized, they literally have not had an opportunity....we should focus on them now....if we don't, they will, or a portion of them will become the predators 15 years from now."

He went on to say, "The consensus is A) we must take back the streets. It doesn't matter whether or not the person that is accosting your son or daughter or my son or daughter, my wife, your husband, my mother, your parents, it doesn't matter whether or not they were deprived as a youth. It doesn't matter whether or not they had no background that enabled them to become socialized into the fabric of society. It doesn't matter whether or not they're the victims of society. The result is they're about to knock my mother on the head with a lead pipe, shoot my sister, beat up my wife, take on my sons."

He used this fear narrative to scare Americans into supporting legislation that would destroy the black community. Yet, they will vote for him in an overwhelming majority. Cory Booker correctly described Biden as an "architect of mass incarceration." Contrast this with Trump who passed justice reform legislation.

In His Own Words

In 1977, after Biden sided with the segregationist, he said, "Unless we do something about this, my children are going to grow up in a jungle, the jungle being a racial jungle with tensions having built so high that it is going to explode at some point. We have got to make some move on this." Typical white flight racist chatter.

In 1975 he said, "I don't feel responsible for the sins of my father and grandfather. I feel responsible for what the situation is today, for the sins of my own generation, and I'll be damned if I feel responsible to pay for what happened 300 years ago." So much for Kamala's reparations.

In 2020 when a black journalist, Errol Barnett, asked if Joe Biden had taken a cognitive test, Biden went off on him, saying, "That's like saying before you got on this program, you're taking a test whether you are taking cocaine or not. What do you think, huh? Are you a junkie?" His go-to for a professional black reporter was to call him a junkie? That old school thought of all blacks being addicted to drugs and raping women cannot help but seep out of Biden's racist pores. Then he went on about how blacks unlike Latinos, are not diverse thinkers, implying that all black people think alike. He views them as a monolith of drug invested criminals that require restrictive laws and harsher sentences for similar crimes as whites.

Besides this, he said, "If you have a problem figuring out whether you're for me or Trump, then you ain't black." Does Joe Biden have the right to tell anyone they are not black? He assumes that all black people think alike and vote alike. Anyone who dares cross Joe losses their race card? Why? Because Joe Biden kissed the ring of Barack Obama? Race is now decided by some old racist white guy? People on the left have been ignoring this for too long. If you stand against racism, then you must stand against Joe Biden. He is the embodiment of the old racist white America.

When running against Mitt Romney in 2012, he said to an all-black church, "They're going to put y'all back in chains." Race-baiting to pander for African-American votes, ignoring the racial division created. This is the type of divisive rhetoric that has given rise to extreme elements burning up our cities.

He implied that poor kids are all non-white. This type of "racial simplification" is textbook racism. While speaking in Iowa he said, "Poor kids are just as bright and just as talented as white kids." In July 2020 he implied that Trump can't hold China accountable for the virus because Americans can't distinguish between individuals from South Korea and Beijing.

He sent out a fund-raising email after the death of George Floyd. It contained a link to donate to the Biden campaign. He did not hesitate to exploit the death of an African-American for political profit.

Is Joe Biden the most racist Democrat alive today? Perhaps, especially considering how "anti-racist" they have become. However, during his 1988 presidential campaign, he spoke of standing up for civil rights on three separate occasions.

"When I marched in the civil rights movement, I did not march with a 12-point program; I marched with tens of thousands of others to change attitudes, and we changed attitudes." Joe Biden did not participate in any marches. On the other hand, he said, "When I was 17 years old, like many of you, I participated in sit-ins to desegregate the restaurants and movie houses of Wilmington, Delaware." Then he said, "I was one of those guys that sat in and marched and all that stuff."

Surely he would have been photographed during such events; however, he was not. Although plenty of pictures show him shaking hands with racist politicians. Why aren't there any pictures of him marching with civil rights leaders? Because it is a lie. He recanted the whole story and dropped out of the 1988 presidential race. He said, "I was not an activist...I was not down in Selma, I was not anywhere else." He failed to gain the Democratic party nomination in 1988 after a scandal broke out, and he was accused of plagiarizing a speech.

The most ironic part of all this is that he picked the narrative back up after being selected VP by Obama. He spoke of coming out of the civil rights movement. Imagine a white guy lying about marching for civil rights. Is this not appalling? Liberals are going to have to hold their nose and close their eyes when they vote in November.

As badly as Joe Biden wants to believe he was some kind of civil rights icon, he was not. He openly lies when confronted with incontrovertible evidence. He was actually working to undermine the black community in the legislature while pandering for their votes in Black Churches.

His racist comments were not simply directed at black people but also Jews. As an example, when speaking at the 40th anniversary celebration for the Legal Services Corporation he referred to his son, Beau Biden, and his Iraq experience. "People would come to him and talk about what was happening to them at home in terms of foreclosures, in terms of bad loans that were being ... I mean these Shylocks who took advantage of, um, these women and men while overseas." Using the Anti-Semitic trope to imply that all bankers are greedy Jewish people. The derogatory term "Shylock" comes from a villain in the Shakespearean Play called The Merchant of Venice. The Anti-defamation league was outraged.

For the Hispanic community he voted for a border fence and said he was proud of it. He also said we should not give amnesty to illegal immigrants and that people who want to immigrate here legally should be required to learn English. He also said some offensive things about Indian Americans, "In Delaware, the largest growth in population is Indian Americans moving from India. You cannot go to a 7-Eleven or a Dunkin' Donuts unless you have a slight Indian accent. I'm not joking." Ironic that he would choose an Afro-American-Indian as a VP.

Lastly, while on the campaign trail in December of 2019 Joe went on a bizarre rant about his days as a lifeguard. "And by the way, you know I sit on the stand and it'd get hot. I got a lot of − I got hairy legs ... that turn blonde in the sun," Biden said. "And the kids used to come up and reach in the pool and rub my leg down so it was straight and then watch the hair come back up again. They'd look at it. So I learned about roaches and I learned about kids jumping on my lap, and I love kids jumping on my lap." This is the uncomfortably side of Joe Biden, the one that likes to sniff people's hair or bite his wife's fingers. Perhaps, it is the side that has caused some people to claim sexual harassment.

Is Biden Sexist?

During the 1991 Anita Hill's testimony, Biden was accused of not supporting or believing her accusations of sexual harassment against Supreme Court nominee Clarence Thomas. Sen. Orrin Hatch said Biden privately confessed to him during the proceedings that he did not believe her. The entire process was a disaster orchestrated by Biden.

Biden said, "As the committee chairman, I take responsibility that she did not get treated well. I take responsibility for that." Anita Hill held on to her bitter feelings for many years to come but said she would support him in the election.

However, Tara Reade said that she would not support him. Biden was accused of sexual assault against her in 1993. A story that was buried by the political establishment and mainstream media, despite Tara being a lifelong Democrat. She claimed a supervisor told her to bring Joe Biden his gym bag and then he pinned her against a wall and sexually assaulted her with his fingers. How can he get away with this? Is the #metoo movement dead? Aren't we supposed to believe her? If it was a Trump accuser we would have wall to wall coverage.

Biden has yet to answer tough cross-examined questions on this topic. In a virtual town hall on MSNBC, when asked what voters should do he said, "I think they should vote their heart, and if they believe Tara Reade, they probably shouldn't vote for me. I wouldn't vote for me if I believed Tara Reade." Joe Biden called on the National Archives to release any records of her complaint and yet crickets.

Seven other women have accused Joe Biden of touching them inappropriately or making them uncomfortable in some way. Many of these women are Democrats and some can be seen on camera. The creepiest one is him petting a little girl's face from behind at a US Senate ceremonial swearing-in in the Old Senate. Smelling people's hair, and commenting on little girls' appearances. Much of it is uncomfortable to watch. His staff has brushed it off saying he is an oblivious toucher.

Biden gave a non-apology apology for some of his actions. Saying, "I'm not sorry for anything that I've ever done." Including when he hugged and put his hand on Caitlyn Caruso's thigh right after she shared a story of sexual assault at the University of Nevada in 2016.

Recently when Biden was asked a tough question by Lyz Lenz at the LGBTQ Presidential Forum in Iowa. Joe Biden used a condescending technique known as "sexism with a smile." She asked him about his stance on don't ask don't tell, and defense of marriage. He replied with "You're a lovely person." Then, later as they were walking off the stage he said, "You're a real sweetheart."

It is one of those things where you could replace lovely with a derogatory word and that is what he felt. Biden has been around in politics long enough to know you cannot say everything you want, but we as Americans are smart enough to know what he meant.

Is it right to put this much pressure on a 77 year old man?

It is hard to comment on how Biden feels about current events because he does not talk much. He takes his time to filter his ideas through political pollsters, then uses speech writers to polish them up before finally reading it off a teleprompter. Sometimes gaffing and reading "top-line message," like during a scripted NBC 6 interview. Who reads off a teleprompter for a one on one interview? This lack of authenticity is a huge problem for voters. He also read, "end of quote," and told one of his minions to "move it up here," referring to the lines on the teleprompter. We are not here to vote against someone but for someone. Hiding in the basement and failing to answer tough questions is not a good political strategy.

Unfortunately, we live in such a polarizing time that Biden still enjoys massive support despite doing nothing to earn it. The debates, if they happen, will be like putting an injured fossil in the ring with an angry Mike Tyson. The political fallout will make it impossible to vote for Biden. The Democrats will do everything in their power to play up the virus so Biden doesn't have to speak in public. Why? Because he says crazy things like "a black man invented the light bulb, not a white guy named Edison."

Later at that same event in Kenosha, Wisconsin he pretended to take questions from the audience but they were pre-approved questions as one person from the audience called him out for it "My name is Portia Bennett. I'm just going, to be honest, Mr. Biden, I was told to go off this paper but I can't. You need the truth, and I'm part of the truth. I was born here, raised here," she continued "I have to give you the truth of the people."

Biden has to be kept to a tight script or he will say bizarre or sad things. Like the time on MSNBC when Biden awkwardly apologized, "That's a stupid way to say that but I really." As Nicolle Wallace forged ahead, "Donald Trump was asked on —" Biden again interrupted, "Sorry." Then Nicolle said, "Go ahead." Biden finished with, "No. No. Probably best I don't."

A candidate should have the confidence to answer simple questions. If he cannot then how does he expect to lead an entire nation? This lack of self-confidence to stand in front of conservative reporters disqualifies Biden from the demanding office of president. How can we expect him to stand up to world leaders when he can't even stand up to Sean Hannity? He needs to step in the ring with a reporter of the opposition or step off the stage.

Moreover, if Biden does not debate, that must be a red-line for us as a nation. We could construct two glass boxes and put Biden in an air filtered chamber, or let him webcam in remotely. The virus is no excuse. We do not need an audience—just two candidates and a moderator. He must not be supported if he does not debate as Nancy Pelosi has advised.

This election will be a test of our democracy. How far to the left has our country gone? It's a lot further than we think. The left has been pushing our country for decades. Slowly pressing their narratives unchecked in our universities and schools, covering for terrible things their politicians do while calling out the opposing side for minor infractions. They ignore the mental decline of Joe Biden while trying to call out Trump as mentally unfit for office.

In May of 2020, Biden said, "I'm prepared to say that I have a record of over 40 years and that I'm going to beat Joe Biden. Look at my record." He apparently forgot that he is Joe Biden on CNBC. Is this man fit to be commander and chief if he cannot even sit down for a softball interview with a liberal news network?

'I released all my medical records,' Biden said. 'But you never know. You never know what's going on. And I'm sure what would happen is I have — some people looking would say, 'Is the person Biden picked capable of, God forbid something happened to Biden, that they would be able to take over immediately?'

This is why the divisive choice of Kamala Harris is so detrimental to his ticket. She is far out of the mainstream on every major issue. To give her the presidency would wreck our nation. Before his choice Biden said, "I can think of at least eight women, at least four or five people of color, that I think are qualified to be vice president of the United States, but for me, it has to be demonstrated that whoever I pick is two things. One is capable of being president because I'm an old guy. No, I'm serious. Look, thank God I'm in great health, I work out, no I'm serious, you know I work out every morning. I'm in good shape." Doctors have been concerned about Biden's risk of stroke because he has an irregular heartbeat and previously suffered aneurysms.

In 1988, Biden had to have emergency brain surgery due to aneurysms, something difficult to fully recover from. Electing Joe Biden would be cruel. He is suffering from some type of cognitive decline. He oftentimes does not know where he is, and he loses his train of thoughts mid-sentence. He confuses his wife with his sister. His gaffes are all over the internet. This is not shyness as the man has been a seasoned politician for over 40 years. The fact that more people are not talking about this is proof of the left-wing dominance in the media.

Joe Biden is past retirement age and incapable of fulfilling the strenuous demands of being commander and chief. Electing him may put us in the uncomfortable position of imposing the 25th amendment. It will be awkward for us as a nation and cruel to Biden as a person. If elected he would be the oldest president ever by a long-shot. Trump is the current record holder at 70 years old. Biden will be 78 in November.

His election would be like forcing an injured man to climb up a tree and chop it down. It is cruel, we need to let him retire in peace. He does not need the glare of the media spotlight going through his disastrous record. This is exactly why the left chose him because he is too weak to stand up to them. He is being propped up by an out of control left-wing agenda. In Biden they feel like they have the perfect empty vessel to fill America with their radical agenda, full of wars and socialism.

Is Joe Biden mean?

At first, Biden seems like a sweet old man but he is not. The media would like us to buy into the harmless Uncle Joe narrative but this type of blind allegiance is dangerous. On several occasions, he has been downright rude to people, especially those who did not fully support him. He told a Detroit autoworker he was "full of s***," when they were discussing gun rights. He then immediately called the guy a liar when the auto worker was outraged about being spoken to disrespectfully.

He was caught on camera telling a Des Moines activist "vote for someone else" after poking the man in the chest and pulling on his jacket. He did this because the man said he would not vote for Biden in the primary but would in the general election. Biden said that he does not care about the general, and he needs the primary votes.

In New Hampshire, a student asked Biden, "So how do you explain the performance in Iowa and why should the voters believe that you can win the national election?" Biden replied, "It's a good question, number one, Iowa is a Democratic caucus. Ever been to a caucus?" to which she indicated yes. "No, you haven't," Biden retorted. "You're a lying dog-faced pony soldier." What a weird rude thing to say to a young impressionable student on the world stage.

Another example was when an 83-year-old man asked him a tough question about being "too old" and the corruption in Ukraine. "We all know Trump has been messing around in Ukraine," the old man said, "You on the other sent your son over there to get a job and work for a gas company and had no experience in natural gas," he said. "You're selling access to the president just like he is." Biden became angry and said, "You're a damn liar, man. That's not true. And no one has ever said that" Biden vexed while menacingly approaching as a staffer tried to take away the microphone.

"Let him go. Let him go," Biden said to the staffer, "the reason I'm running is because I've been around a long time and I know more than most people know and I can get things done. And that's why I'm running." Biden then challenged the man saying, "Let's do push-ups together here, man. Let's run. Let's do whatever you want to do. Let's take an IQ test." After more tense exchanges Biden replied, "You said I set up my son to work on an oil company," Biden continued. "Isn't that what you said? Get your words straight, Jack!" Biden was very agitated and said, "You don't hear that on MSNBC! You did not hear that at all. Look, I'm not going to get into an argument with you, man." Then the man replied, "You don't have any more backbone than Trump does," the man declared, "Well, I'm not voting for you," Then Biden replied, "Well, I knew you weren't. You're too old to vote for me."

Later Biden said, "I didn't lose my temper. You want to see my temper, keep going," Biden continued, "I didn't lose my temper. What I wanted to do was shut this down." Why would he want to shut down a conversation about his son and Ukraine? What about China?

Is Joe Biden Corrupt?

The media has created a myth that it is somehow unethical to speak of Hunter Biden as if he is a small child. He is a 50-year-old man that sells influence on the world stage. He collects checks for his father's political accomplishments. It is not in our interest to turn a blind eye to it.

Right out of school, Hunter Biden got a high paying job at MBNA in Delaware, a bank that contributed heavily to his father's campaign. Later he started a lobbying firm to lobby congress, where his dad worked in the Senate. Records indicate that on two separate occasions Joe Biden reached out to the Department of Justice and Department of Homeland Security about issues that his son was lobbying for.

In 2006, Hunter was appointed to the board of Amtrak by George W. Bush, probably a political favor for his father's vote in favor of the Iraq war and the Patriot Act. One story did make its way out in the public eye a little, and that is Ukraine.

Why would Hunter Biden get a job in Ukraine? He knows little about energy, doesn't speak the language, and does not live there. Yet, he was placed on the board of Burisma Holdings, a corrupt natural gas company facing money laundering charges. In an interview, Hunter said that if his last name had not been Biden, then he probably would not have been appointed to the board.

Joe Biden bragged about the whole thing in 2016 at the Council of Foreign Relations. He claimed to have gone to Ukraine as VP to announce a billion-dollar loan guarantee and said if the Burisma Holdings prosecutor was not fired, then the money would be cut off. He used American taxpayer funds to hold a foreign government hostage for the benefit of his son's bank account.

It worked and the prosecutor was fired. The prosecutor claimed he was fired solely because of his involvement in the investigation of Burisma Holdings. The media covered for Biden by saying that the prosecutor was corrupt without ever providing evidence of his previous corruption. His only crime was investigating a company that Hunter Biden collected large checks from.

Contrast this with the standard set for the Trump family. They lost international businesses because of their political office. They live under a 24-hour media microscope. Meanwhile, the Biden family gets rich off Joe's political clout, and for some reason, we fail to prosecute them over it.

It doesn't stop there, the even bigger issue involves China. A nation that is growing on the international stage by leaps and bounds. They have become our top rival and are taking an ever more aggressive posture. They are building islands and converting them into military bases, creating drone armies, and crushing resistance in places like Hong Kong. They are networking with bad actors like North Korea, Iran, and Russia. They have enslaved Muslims and crushed alleged criminals with little due process. They are the world's top executioner, and many of their citizens lack basic freedoms.

They have a terrible human rights track record with 500 million Chinese living on less than $2 a day and 30 million people living in caves. Massive pollution and terrible drinking water plague the country. Until 2015, they regulated childbirth and forced sterilizations. They lack basic freedoms like speech and the right to bear arms. If you speak badly about the Chinese government you will be punished. This is important for Americans who want to do business in China. The NBA, for illustration, makes millions of TV deals with the Chinese. Therefore their social justice campaign has been silent on the Muslim slave camps.

The Chinese understand who to pay off. They know which groups will weaken us by sowing division among our people. They are avid supporters of BLM, and whoever else wants to destroy America. They see how this poisonous seed can divide our people in hopes of dethroning us. China has openly said that they want to replace America as the lone superpower.

Listening to Joe Biden you get a much different understanding of China. According to him, China is not a danger to us, they are not an enemy. He said, "A rising China is a positive development, not only for the people of China but for the people of the United States and the world as a whole." This public statement directly contradicts what was going on behind the scenes on the world stage. Biden was appointed the lead on China and refused to identify them as one of our greatest threats.

Why then would Joe Biden say such nice things about them? To find the answer we have to go back to 2013 when he met with Chinese officials and brought his son. Why would he bring his son on a diplomatic trip? The media has never asked, they were too busy basking in the glow of Obama. Ten days after Joe Biden's trip, Hunter Biden's investment firm BHR (Shanghai) Equity Investment Fund Management had a 1 billion dollar private equity deal with the Chinese government. Did they pay this money in hopes of winning political favors? Or was it for kind words? Or worse yet for American military secrets?

Whatever the reason, it seems to have worked for the Chinese. Paying off the NBA and powerful Democratic establishment, silences the media and everyday people ignore China. Take it a step further and get the media to shout, "RUSSIA RUSSIA RUSSIA," and you have a good political strategy to overtake America on the world stage.

China did not petal that money for free, they wanted something. What they got was a swamp creature named dirty Joe Biden. Here is a man that sold out his country for a billion dollars, politics for money. Close your eyes and hope you do not destroy our nation. There is a lot more dirt to this story, enough to fill an entire book.

The bottom line is, Joe Biden is beholden to our greatest adversary. To this day he refuses to say anything disparaging about the regime, despite their numerous human rights abuses. Is he a coward? Or has he been bought off? If elected, he will ignore America's interest and let China run wild. Biden is too weak to lead us against China.

Also, Biden is in bed with Wall Street to the tune of $44 million compared to Trump's $9 million. After collection hundreds of thousands of dollars at a fundraiser Biden said, "You're putting me in a position to be able to be very competitive," thanking his Wall Street supporters.

The Biden Vessel Theory

Joe Biden will not stand up to the radicals in his party. He will cave to their every demand. He doesn't have the youth and vigor to quell their rebellion. The far-left Democrats choose him for their ambition. In him, they see a vessel that they could float all their ideas on.

This is dangerous because we do not know whose insane ideas will be implemented. Will the Green New Deal pass by executive action? Or through our legislature with its business destroying regulations? Will Biden be able to stand up to AOC and the rest of the DNC? So far, he has caved to their joint task force compromise.

Twenty years ago he might have told the radical wing to sit down, but now nobody stands up to them so they grow stronger. Sensible Democrats are too power-starved to risk fracture. So they will ride the wave thinking it will help them gain control. Instead of using common sense to solve problems they use political allegiances. They group up into their victim classes then hand out symbolic gestures to keep everyone happy, rampaging through our streets tearing down statues.

The extreme left has become obnoxious. They must be hidden from view. When independent news sources cover the acts of burning bibles and flags in our cities, people are repulsed. When they allegedly killed a Trump supporter named Bernell Trammell in broad daylight in Milwaukee, for having the wrong political belief, it was ignored. His life black life did not matter. One would think someone being shot and killed in the heat of election season might be newsworthy. Of course, anything that does not achieve more votes must be squelched. Including when David Dorn was killed in St. Louis trying to stop rioters from breaking into a pawn shop.

Joe Biden is an empty vessel for this insanity. In exchange for power, he will complete the missions they give him. These things, no matter how well-intended they may seem, will lead to a total break-down of society. We will turn into a post-apocalyptic hell hole; if these ideas are left unchecked. Defunding the police, for one thing, will only lead to more crime, fewer people to respond to 911 calls, less training for officers, and fewer qualified officers. Thus creating more of what is supposed to be stopped. The insanity will be so destructive that our cities will be impossible to live in.

They think that all these ideas will make for a peaceful Utopia, but it will have the opposite effect. It is not the intention of the left that is sour, it is the result. For example, welfare is a well-intended program designed to fix the poverty gap. However, after years and years of welfare, the program has not reduced the percentage of poor people. It's always the output of the left that falls short. That is why they must control the media. They must not allow you to see the results of their ideas. If we only see the well-intended input without ever examining the results, then we are more likely to support them.

Biden's Wishful Thinking

Biden has this kind of way about him where he dreams up things that help him politically than he kind of wishes they were true. In particular, he wished he finished in the top half of his law class because it sounds good. He also wishes he did not get caught plagiarizing a speech because it sounds bad. Moreover, he wishes he was a civil rights icon. He lives out this fantasy in front of people all the time. He wishes he was arrested for trying to see Nelson Mandela in prison. He even went so far as to imagine Mandela thanked him for getting arrested.

In Detroit on September 9, 2020, he said, "Every single thing I talk about, I pay for, by making sure, for the first time, the wealthy begin to pay what they should be paying," Biden continued, "We're not going to punish anybody. No one making under $400,000, which is more money than I've ever made, is going to have to pay more taxes." Biden has made over $15 million since leaving his post as VP. He wishes he was still Middle-Class Joe because it might earn him more votes. Additionally, this is doubly dishonest because how can he pay for the Unity Task Force recommendations if he does not raise taxes? Which is he lying about: Taxes or the Task Force?

He wishes Trump was responsible for the virus and all the 190,000 deaths. Democrats keep trying to pin this on Trump. How can we fault him for a virus that started in China? They attack his response and yet offer no alternatives. They would not have instituted a travel ban. The truth is nobody saw the virus coming and it has been a difficult thing for every nation on Earth to deal with.

Biden wishes the virus made it impossible for him to debate Trump because he knows he would lose. The man cannot stand up to a liberal reporter much less anyone from the opposition. A fair-minded moderator will make him look foolish with all his contradictions.

He wishes all the rioters and looters were somehow Trump supporters. Somehow Biden wants to blame Trump for what is going on in Democrat-run-cities. Americans are not biting on it because we see the DA's and Mayors refusing federal assistance and pulling back the police. Trump does not want to use the extreme Insurrection Act and call in the military.

He wishes he predicted the 9/11 attacks. For some odd reason, he goes around telling people he did. He wishes his silver star story was completely true especially when he follows it up with, "It's the God's truth, my word as a Biden." Heavy words for somebody not being completely honest and mixing three stories into one.

He wishes he did not call for spending cuts to Social Security, Medicare, and Welfare. He wished it so hard he lied to Bernie Sanders hoping it was true. Some people may have thought it was until audio of him advocating for it was published.

He wishes we could not vote in person, so the waters could be muddied with mail-in ballots. We may be on the verge of a large-scale coup attempt. It is ridiculous, if Nancy Pelosi can get her hair done in a salon with no mask then kids can go to school and people can vote.

Ticket Conclusion

Voting against Trump is no reason to vote for Biden/Harris who are corrupt and racist. Biden against black people, Harris against white people. It is symbolic of the "Democratic switch" so many on the left lament about. Before the 1964 Civil Rights Bill, Democrats were openly racist and mingled with the KKK. The switch happened not with racism but with races. The new Democrats are now racist against white people.

That was the "big switch," now we have a new breed of liberals that hate cops, white people, and anyone who wears a MAGA hat. How can you hate someone you have never met? Or hate someone for choosing a law enforcement career path? The world is not that simple. All police officers are not corrupt, and all white people are not evil. The truth is more nuanced than that. There are good people and bad people everywhere in society, including in these so-called 'peaceful protests.'

Many of our people have been brainwashed by vile propaganda. The accusations of racist were only meant to win an election, not something to build a life around. These poor people are taught to speak of systemic racism, which has made certain lives impossible to live. They somehow believe people are terrorized by other people they have never met. This type of fear-mongering is the same card racist whites used against innocent blacks. They maligned an entire race of people for something they cannot control, their skin color.

Now they demonize Caucasians, viewing them as weak and pathetic. An easy prey that can be vilified and destroyed. Giving these people power will only stifle our efforts for a just and color blind society, one where people are judged based on who they are not who their parents were. We should not demonize people who have racist great-grandparents.

Harris and Biden are both spreaders of this demented propaganda. Both are for sale, and will financially profit from their political power, whether it be through children, public speaking tours, or massive contributions. Speaking tours should be made illegal. Paying a politician hundreds of thousands of dollars after leaving their office for saying a few things in front of employees is a total political sham. These politicians are being bribed for political favors while in office and then paid after they leave. Favors, we as taxpayers, end up footing the bill for.

6

Bernie and the Radical Left

Sanders

Bernie Sanders is a friendly conman who sells everything for the low price of nothing. If you think this is a good deal, chances are that you feel a burning sensation, but that sensation is not your passion for the victim class—it is the logical half of your mind catching fire because of the hot corner you shoved it in. Free healthcare, free college tuition, and free welfare are hardly free and have nothing to do with freedom.

Senator Sanders is dangerous because he is a cancer dressed up like Santa Clause. Where cancer is a disease that causes one group of cells to horde all the nutrients, and grow out of control, consequently killing the entire body, and Santa Clause is the old white guy that gives you free stuff.

Socialism run-a-muck is cancer, caused by a desire to feed the underprivileged cells that are growing out of control. This is accomplished by feeding them from the mouths of more successful cells. Sanders wants to tear down the fabric of free enterprise under the title of income inequality. This is just a fancy way of saying you are going to steal from one group to give to another.

He wants to achieve this by transforming into a giant bird and chomping up all the corporations, then regurgitating them to the hapless victims of the underclass. The problem with feeding people intravenously through the government is that the needy will grow and not shrink. I have personally heard students as young as 12 and 13 say that they have no desire for education. "Why should I work and learn when I can just live off the government?" You cannot stop that mentality; it will spread like a disease, consuming our cities.

It is born out of a humanitarian attempt to even things out, but the unintended consequence is that the cells that were supposed to slough off end up growing and dominating. That is a lot of what goes on in our country with Tent Cities. People fed by spare change and government handouts have grown to blocks of homeless crowding the city streets and cutting off the flow of traffic.

The more money that is thrown at the problem, the worse it becomes. It is a trap, and trying to stop it is difficult because the truth like this is shouted down as some type of "ist." My only goal is to help society if you can prove that adding more money to the pot would fix anything. I would be all for it. However, the truth is it does not. Feeding a cat in the back alley only multiplies the number of cats you have.

While it may make our heart feel all warm and fuzzy to feed that stray cat, the simple fact is that we are not helping reduce the number of stray cats. The co-dependent cat might have a litter or invite friends over. Now we have more stray cats to feed, and the more we feed them, the more we will have. It is an endless cycle that could have been prevented by teaching the cat how to hunt or simply allowing nature to run its course.

Feeding the homeless is no solution— nor is giving them spare change. The solution is to teach them how to become productive members of society. We use the carrot of educational opportunity to provide them with a chance to learn a skill, and we use the stick of a cold hard reality. Failing to capitalize on one's chances will lead to a life without shelter or basic necessities. This type of motivation will help more people achieve success. It embraces the aforementioned normal distribution seen throughout the natural world.

Giving free handouts will only make the line longer, and instead of people spending time and energy on becoming more skilled or productive, they will focus on improving their place in the line. The more you give, the more you will have to give, until our entire society crumbles under the weight of our leftist "generosity." Wealth redistribution weakens the bonds of a nation.

Free things taken from other people may sound great until we unmask the pockets we are digging in. The American taxpayers drive the economic engine. Taking from them slows down the wheels of progress and weakens us all.

Getting free college tuition sounds great, but is it fair to hand the bill off to the next generation? Would we be better off as a nation if we had more college-educated citizens? Maybe so, and perhaps there are legitimate arguments to be made, but how we get there is important.

We do not want to end up with a society full of unskilled workers begging for a fair minimum wage. How is that right? Forcing someone to pay a higher wage for an unqualified worker will only create fewer jobs and more unskilled applicants. We reward people that lack basic motivation. The wrong message is sent to the youth, which says, "Forget about school; all you have to do is support Senator Sanders, and you will get a living wage." There is no work ethic required—simply press a button in a voting booth. It is an easy way out, and many more people will take it.

The more you feed it, the more it will grow. Why should anyone go to college for four years when you could make $15 an hour right out of junior high? Of course, Sanders wants to feed the poor minimum wage cat. The only problem is all the unintended consequences. We must allow failure to be a motivator.

Medicare for all is a great sentiment but how do we afford the $1.4-3.2 trillion a year price tag? Is this much growth in governance going to make us stronger? Improve our freedom? The government will have to raise taxes— the working class will pay more. Is that fair? Is healthcare a fundamental right of being a citizen? Or, is it something to strive for? Perhaps a motivating factor when given an educational opportunity. It gives weight to the notion, "Get an education because your life depends on it."

Senator Sanders is not above milking the racial justice, going so far as to be irrational to prove that he is a card-carrying member. This is the most concerning feature of these types of leftists—they become racist against white people just to prove that they are not racist against people of color. At a Democratic Debate Senator Sanders said: "When you are white, you do not know what it is like to be living in a ghetto. You do not know what it is like to be poor. You do not know what it is like to be hassled when you walk down the street or when you get dragged out of a car." The implication is that we live in this homogeneous society with all blacks living in the ghetto and all whites living in the affluent areas. This is simply not true, plenty of white people live in poor neighborhoods and plenty of black people live in affluent areas. It is a racist attempt to play to the racist victim mind-set.

In all honesty, a great deal of hyperbole is required to create the injustices necessary for "action." Stories need to be specially crafted by the leftist journalists to ensure maximum emotional outrage, thus playing to the narrative of systemic racism. The more this narrative is reinforced, the stronger the action and the more political gain people like Sanders get.

Does he really care about the plight of the impoverished? Perhaps, in his mind, but he does not take the necessary or logical steps to truly improve their lives. He is not willing to take away the excuses and deny the handouts. He is not willing to be the strong leader that offers discipline over enabling. Instead, he acts like a parent overfeeding a child. The codependency is sickening.

Sanders gets votes; the victim class gets free handouts. This symbiosis creates a cancer that will kill our society, if not for the radiation of capitalist truth.

NAGS (Not A Good Strategy)

Knowing the right time to do something requires a certain level of maturity lacking from radicals on the far-left. Knowing what campaign strategies are good and which are bad will help liberals gracefully regain control of their party.

- Labeling everyone you disagree with as racist is NAGS.
- Going to get your hair done after putting the world on lockdown is NAGS.
- Manipulating a virus panic to destroy the economy is NAGS.
- Accusing Trump of killing 190,000 Americans is NAGS.
- Infiltrating the FBI to try and tear down a political opponent is NAGS.
- Electing someone solely based on their identity is NAGS.
- Opening our borders and offering free everything to everybody is NAGS.
- Murdering someone in Portland for their political beliefs is NAGS .
- A large crowd bragging about it afterwards is indefensible.
- Ignoring the violence or egging it on in is NAGS.
- Trying to burn down historic St John's church near the White House is NAGS.
- Hiding in the basement and avoiding real questions is NAGS.
- Threatening executive action on the 2nd amendment is NAGS.
- Silencing the opposition by boycotts and bans is Not American!
- Manipulating sensational headlines to motivate radicals is NAGS.
- Throwing a temper tantrum after an election because you lost is NAGS.

Trying to create chaos and destroy the country is not a good campaign strategy. The left comes off looking like a vision-less sore loser. Protesters are questioned about why they are protesting and offer silence. They ignore rebuttals and scream slogans. For the sake of our democracy the left must show basic integrity. Instead of tearing down, cultivate a new vision for the direction of our country. Then try to win over more people with great ideas. The Republicans do not hold a monopoly on truth. It is just that Democrats have surrendered any attempt at meaningful debate, instead opting for rage.

There is no logic to their anger; they scream Nazis scum at Jewish Trump supporters. They knowingly burn down black businesses in the name of racial justice. White liberals stop a black woman on her way to work to stop racial injustice. They collaborated with foreign powers to create a fake dossier, to accuse Trump of collaborating with a foreign power. They started an investigation in search of a crime and convicted people of unrelated crimes. It should have more blow-back from logically fair-minded people. They need to stop trying to jail political opponents.

The Misguided Media

The out of control fake news media has brainwashed a generation of the leftist electorate. Words like "racist" and "sexist" make them rage around on Twitter. It feels good to have their feelings reinforced. Lies brought about by a false sense of reality become a dopamine-like addiction.

The yellow journalist is the supplier built with all the necessary low ethical standards, pushing sensational headlines designed to smack the reader's attention. Violence appeals to our most primal instincts like tabloid junk food for our brains.

They let the agenda drive the story. Pushing for facts to support their preconceived notions. They have no integrity, only a pill to push. They let the emotions of the moment outweigh the parameters of the story. They are political drug dealers disguised as news reporters. They label protest as "mostly peaceful" despite 19 dead people, $2 billion in damage, and 14,000 arrested.

Unnamed sources scour the headlines. Stories are built by an overeager press bent on ending the presidency of a duly elected representative. Democratic supporters are too ignorant to detect it, or too foolish to hold them accountable. United in a war, they see victory as more important than integrity. They will do nothing to divide the troops because their politics are based on tribes of people and not principles.

The journalist should collect facts organically like raindrops, and then use all the water to drive a true narrative. Dedicated non-partisan reporters printing a story based solely on empirical evidence—imagine that. It is time to break the cycle of addiction and demand integrity—cleansing our minds of this toxic pollutant.

However, these facts have trouble resonating over the deep-seated emotions the mainstream media has planted in a significant portion of the electorate. Citizens turning hysterical and resorting to violence in our city streets. Emotional breakdowns and homemade bombs are being thrown in Portland's "mostly peaceful protest." Seattle turned into an occupied war zone with the Democratic media dishonestly calling it the "Summer of love." The left-wing machine ran a smear campaign on the federal officers in Portland. As if the federal agents trying to keep an angry mob from burning down a courthouse are somehow to blame for a group of anarchist agitators bent on destroying our "filthy" nation.

Agreements were made so that the police would patrol the courthouse, and what happened? The angry mob still runs around burning things. Rioting for 100 straight nights and counting. Nobody on the left has enough courage to stop them. They deny federal support from Trump, knowing how messy the Insurrection Act would be with our military in a city full of anarchists. People will die.

Twisting people for partisan gains has long-lasting negative consequences. Some people see through the lies and turn on their captors' others seek to destroy the system and hurt millions in their quest. Democracy requires an enlightened electorate capable of avoiding contagious groupthink. We are not enemies of each other. We have to educate each other. We have to set aside our special interest and focus on the general interest. Stop trying to do things for a segregated group of the population, and start doing things that benefit everyone as a whole. Every action the Democratic party takes has one sole purpose: political gain for themselves. They rarely act in the general interest of all people. They have no interest in uniting us because the division is their power source.

They have gone so far left Ted Kopple calls them out. It would take a full-length documentary to expose it all. We could produce it under the title Free the Press. An example of this would be the biases surrounding recent mass shootings. If it fits the narrative of a white male with an "assault rifle," then we are inundated with calls for repealing the second amendment.

This left-wing ideology plays out in seemingly innocent ways by claiming to protect the victims, but what they are really trying to protect is their agenda. We never seem to hear from the pro-second amendment victims. Do they exist?

Mass shootings are terrible tragedies that should never be used as political ploys. Yet ever the opportunist, the left uses them to galvanize against the right. The shooters are pawns fed fame for their deeds of destruction. Emboldened by the mainstream media they put infamy over their own life.

As a society, we must agree to take the spotlight off of these individuals. It is the only way to deprive them of what they want most— to feel noticed, important, or fixed by whatever is missing from their broken minds.

We should make it an unlegislated rule—never show the killer's face or mention his/her name. The same type of thing we do for victims of sexual abuse. The simple fact is we cannot prevent all tragedies and taking away people's rights is counter-productive. There will always be violence and there will always be people selling the miracle cure: safety for freedom.

Our partisan press has taken over the realm of comedy. This weird fusion between news and late-night jesters gives leftists an unchallenged approach to gain support for their ideas. They promote a point of view then retreat behind the "only a comedian label." Many of these comedians are nothing more than camouflaged political operatives. They received massive backlash for "normalizing' Trump.

The media has a bright light and refuses to shine it on things they disagree with politically. They manipulate stories by tone, syntax, emphasis, and style, to subjugate a large group of Americans against another group. This separation will become permanent without detoxification. It is dangerous to lie and separate our people. We may disagree on many things, but we need our moments of unity.

The Far-Left

Leftist control begins by planting the seeds of utopia. They promise their socialist agenda will cure all the ills of modern society. Give them power and they will end suffering, specifically poverty and racism. They build a base of support by uniting the basic human desire to help with the desperation of impoverished citizens. They convince massive hordes of people their day to day struggles can be solved by reaching into the pocketbooks of billionaires. Like a Snake Oil Salesman, they promise the magic cure for the harsh facts of reality.

They hate the normal distribution and its bell-shaped curve, instead, they want everyone to win. They live in a fantasy classroom where everyone can make an A+. This is a broken idea that does not work, people have to fail. The world is meant to have millionaires and homeless. Trying to take one group's money to lift up another group will only increase the likely-hood of system failure.

They speak of how the current system must be destroyed so that theirs can be installed. They never pause to look back at the wake of destruction they leave, only clamoring for more and more power. A society that feeds off its economic engine will surely crumble. Taking money from other people is like taking blood from the human body. One can be taxed a little and still make a living but there is a point at which it becomes impossible to survive. Listening to liberals talk about 80% tax brackets should alarm us all. This will not only destroy our economic engine but it would create a system of dependents.

The left rationalizes lying for the greater good; it is a necessary sacrifice for the utopic vision. Nothing breaks away the plaque of these lies like the cold hard truth. Ideas that counter their narrative and undermine their belief system make them look like fools. This triggers them into censoring opposing viewpoints, instead of being humble and reshaping their vision.

The far-left looks down upon everything including reality. They have an absolute belief in their vision of politics. If things do not add up then reality must be wrong because they cannot be. They have been known to come up with "theories" on why 2 + 2 does not equal 4. Irrational positions become the norm mandated by social control like that of a childhood bully. In tight-knit clusters, they maintain growth by putting their fingers in their ears and ignoring reason. They begin to coalesce around cancel culture. The politically correct culture keeps the flock in line, ignoring moral codes like taking other people's money is wrong.

The left craves political power and control. Like a festering cancer, they seek to dominate the body of governance. Spreading from one branch to the next. Starved and screaming if they are not fed. They fill up our city streets demanding to be heard, demanding change but never offer a coherent direction in which we are to change.

What they want is power, money, and control. If people have to die then so be it. If riots improve Democratic chances then we need more anger. If the polls dip then we need to calm down. They play an ignorant populace like an orchestra, feeding talking point memos to anchors who parrot the exact phrases on multiple channels. For example, "impeachable offense," "manufactured crisis," or "reimagine policing." Over and over again until the audience gets the talking point down so well they could probably run for office.

The left has lost their big picture message; the only thing that unites them is their hatred for Donald Trump. Why? They hate how successful he is and how popular he is with his base. They do not respect him as a president or as a person. They believe he is a deplorable lowlife incapable of higher thought. If he likes Hydroxychloroquine then they hate it. Does not matter how many more people die, in fact, more death and chaos are good if they help Joe Biden.

Religion as Politics

The far left has strung together an interconnected web of lies so tight it has created a religion out of politics. Replacing Christianity with a political-religious ideology based on identity and social justice. Ignoring reason the same way ISIS does.

Indoctrination begins with the original sin: America is an irredeemably racist nation built on stolen Native American land. They ignore the fact that history is littered with nations conquering and enslaving other nations. Even the Native Americans wondered around conquering other tribes. They had some of the most brutal regimes in human history, especially the Aztecs sacrificing millions to their "crop gods." But in the titled mind of a leftest, the US is seen as the sole perpetrator. They ignore the fact that every single country in existence today has conquered the land they live on. The entire earth is composed of nations that have "stolen" their land.

Actually, if the British had not settled in America then we would have never revolted and freedom would not have been born in 1776. We might still be living under the rule of British Royalty. Hundreds of years could have slipped by before self-governance took root. This would undoubtedly undercut the major human innovation of the past century. Cars, phones, moon landings, all of it gone. Our science would probably still be in the dark ages.

As Americans we have shown great kindness to our indigenous people, giving them solitary reservations within our borders. This is not the markings of a cruel inhuman society. It makes us unique in the brutal context of history. It is not healthy to go around riling people up with bitter wars of the past. We need to focus on peace and prosperity.

Within certain circles, political correctness controls them like Joseph Stalin's Soviet Union but have replaced Ukrainian peasants with white males. Evil things said about an entire race are acceptable. When the mind is bent like this, even concrete facts can be ignored. As much as they deserved to be demonized, liberals are still Americans. They have the best of intentions (x), but their thoughts and emotions have been hijacked and manipulated for a political function (f(x)). We must do our best to save them while combating their destructive output (y).

The implementation of the Marxist Postmodernist ideology necessitates the angst of one group over another. The opposition is villainized to the point they cannot be tolerated. This creates an emotional tidal-wave designed to tightly seal the cult. They take their anger of injustice out on the opposition with such vitriol, they can overcome the basic human rejection of cruel actions.

The Nazi's pitted Germans against Jews. They villainized the Jewish people constantly blaming them for their lack of success. The same way the left blames whites for the lack of success of minorities. When the great depression hit they blamed it on the Jews. Using this type of targeting was very powerful. It started a movement with massive parades and passionate leaders. Soon after the world would get a taste of just how full of hatred they were. Jewish children were murdered in the street and it was not even given a second thought. People were routinely forced to do the Nazi salute and chant "Heil Hitler!" to demonstrate compliance.

Today we have Democrats blaming the virus on Trump. We also have out of control mobs demanding people say "black lives matter," and raise their fist in solidarity. The same tight-nit groupthink of Nazism is on display, that blind belief in the cause. In Washington DC a group of mostly white kids barged into a restaurant and said, "we ask you to raise your hand up in the air in solidarity with all black and brown murdered by the police. We demand you to abolish the police." They got in people's faces and demanded "justice."

This mental path is dangerous and must end. Reasonable conversations about police reform are welcomed and necessary. However, barging in on people, burning down buildings, looting stores, and killing people is not reasonable. There is no excuse for violence and anyone who justifies it must be ostracized.

The parishioners of the left buy into the good vs evil narrative and rail against the oppressive satanic system. They embrace the extremists in the BLM/Antifa movements, who target the cops and Trump supporters. Trump/Cops are considered heretics, unworthy of basic human decency. They are turned into evil creatures with their MAGA hats symbolizing hate and oppression like the bloody white hoods of the KKK.

Conservatives must be silenced and destroyed at all costs. Dox their families protest outside their homes. Get them fired from their jobs. By any means necessary they must be silenced. This is war and in war there are casualties. The only idea is the purification of belief through the eradication of opposition. Thousands of people suffering in lockdowns without jobs are just the heads on the Aztec block being sacrificed for the heavenly vision of socialism.

Critical race theory is their word of God. It has spread throughout our universities and seeped into our porous government. It has even shown up in elementary classrooms. They call it diversity training. The idea is that we are a nation of white supremacists and all white people must bow down and repent for their pale skin color. Hollywood has done its part to turn straight white males into serial killers. Even the FBI participates in diversity training. Employees being sent to education camps, and writing apology letters to people they have never met. This type of brainwashing poses a clear and present danger to our nation. Trump created a Patriotic Education Commission to combat racist Anti-American propaganda.

Racism has become the rallying cry of the left. It means to shut off anyone speaking and put them in a mental hate box. It is an easy way to ensure fresh crops of young minds are not lost to conservative truths. Racism represents the most egregious of all sins, and racist should not only be ignored or destroyed. They have bloodguilt in their veins handed down to them by their great-great-grandparents.

They chase racist narratives around like swatting at flies. Racism is suffering from over-usage. Reminiscent of the little boy who cried wolf, when actual racism occurs half the audience is lost. It must end and we all must support the end of its overuse. This gives cover to actual racist and it disrespects early African-Americans who suffered enormously. Mislabeling upstanding Republicans as racist only makes eyes roll. It should be reserved for people who outwardly vocalize their disdain for people of different races. Not overused by some spoiled NASCAR driver claiming someone put a noose in his garage.

We must not allow ourselves to be segregated or divided for any reason. Especially not on something as silly as the melanin in our skin. To suggest that we are somehow different because it is foolish. The difference in the Asian, Black, Latino, and White communities are all based on the cultural differences in these groups. It is a mimicking behavior of humans kind of like that of a color-changing lizard. Compare a black person, raised in a "white environment" and a white person raised in a "black environment" and nine times out of ten you will find they blend in with their environment.

It is all about culture. Do you respect the family? Do you attend church? Do you have a job? Do you respect other people's freedom? Being a good person has nothing to do with skin color and everything to do with cultural values. In our world anyone can be successful; it starts with a good home-life full of opportunity. Our inner cities are full of amazing music and authentic food, but we miss these experiences because crime has become so toxic we cannot interact with each other. It is a great tragedy that certain neighborhoods become no-go zones after dark.

If we start obsessing over skin color and demonizing white people we will end up in a Hitler-esk Germany with whites replacing Jews. Or the majority will grow irritated and we end up back in the racist south. Tribalism is a dangerous game and it is best to set the pendulum to the middle and walk away. Color blind is the only truth, but liberals will never let go of their power source.

Wealth redistribution via over-taxation has become the new charity. The unfairness of it all must be ignored. Money filtered through a biased bureaucracy creates tension that the left feeds off of. Government programs designed to temporarily give people a helping hand end up becoming a way of life.

When you allow people to feed off a system you create a system of feeders, instead of a system of producers. People no longer concern themselves with how to improve their job skills but how to better improve their position in the welfare line. They trade in their votes for the promise of a bigger check. This is the sick sort of bribery that takes place.

Hollywood elites are the clergy standing behind their awkward podiums making grand sermons about how terrible middle America is. The best way to lure someone into a cult is by convincing them they are somehow irredeemable. The guilt narrative is blasted to a fever pitch at their crowded sermons. Their ideas spread feeding off the self-conscious nature of humans. Overcompensation leads to hatred of anyone outside the protected class.

In their religious-political ideology, the underprivileged classes are the diverse chosen people. The liberal politicians have become saint-like-prophets speaking truth to racist power, and Obama is the chosen one. Safe spaces are the holy grounds, and the internet is a bastion of sin and must be censored and purified by the tech giants because converts might be lost. Our system of governance must be destroyed because it is full of racist white slaveholders. Marxism is the ancient text everything is built on. It all starts by defunding the great obstacle known as the police and ends with destroying the infidels, known as conservatives.

7

Systems of Governance

The System

Fringe groups are becoming more and more powerful. Once unheard of entities like the 1619 project, BLM, and Antifa have been growing rapidly. Some people just want to be part of a cause, they grew up envious of the 1960's civil rights movement. What they do not realize is this movement will spawn an oppressive system, built on equity of outcomes, which takes the race of its subjects into account. Reminiscent of the old racist one we had to tear down. History will look upon these groups as villains.

In mathematical terms, these people that desire (x) equity do not understand that it will lead to tyranny (y). Their well intended goal (x) is to fix the output (y) of an entire society. However, all of us have different inputs (x) because we are all unique. Thus, in order to get equal $(y\text{-values})$ one must create a system $(f(x))$ that auto-corrects all the $(x\text{-values})$. This changing system $(f(x))$ is necessarily going to lift-up unsuccessful groups up while pushing-down successful groups. Eliminating the most powerful and beautiful "Normal Distribution," which creates a bell-shaped-curve and exist throughout nature, and turn it into a 'Uniform Distribution," a flat-line constant distribution, which represents maximum entropy, and death.

Why does it cause death? It takes away the incentive to succeed in life. We know that regardless of our input (x) we will get a quota driven output (y). People will lose faith in an inherently bent system $(f(x))$. The programmers of the system will put their favored group as the greatest beneficiary, and justify it by digging up past racial regressions. They ultimately want reparations, taking the money from one tribe and depositing it into the bank account of another. This is not justice, freedom, or the American way. We do not take money from people based on bloodguilt. People are only punished for their choices. We must take a stand.

Instead they should focus on the cultural input (x) because it is far easier to change than reality (z). Where z is a variable that we are only beginning to understand. This strategy is being proposed by people who reject math. They want to look down at a racially divided bar-graph on poverty and feel good about themselves. Ignoring the complete disorder they have created by building a system that necessarily discriminates. This is not the way evolution or mathematics works. Many understand this and just want to create a system (f(x)) that is designed to burn. Anarchy, then from the rubble they will gain control and usher in a new era of domination.

Instead of redesigning reality (z) they need to focus on a shift in culture. Create one that builds people up and offers amazing job skills. The business world is ripe with opportunity. Stop tribalizing people into racial groups, uphold color blind as the gold standard. That means there is no more "white communities" or "black communities," instead we are all "one community." Help everyone succeed except for those that refuse. Let them suffer, let them be the tail end of the normal distribution. There is nothing we can do about the natural tendency of people to make F's and go to jail. Trying to prevent it will make everyone an F, not everyone an A. When the function is manipulated it can breakdown the entire machine (f(x)) and everyone will be an "F." It creates a flat-line Uniform Distribution and humanity will cease to exist.

Cops & Riots

The absurdity of the left plays out in the realm of cops and guns. Leftists, who tend to distrust the police, want to live in a world where only the government has guns. Disarm the common civilian and we will all be victims to the overreaching armed police. Beyond that, they encouraged violent riots then blamed Trump as if we are too stupid to realize. Kamala Harris and the mainstream media fanned the flames using divisive rhetoric too emotionally charge civilians.

Certain criminals create chaotic situations during police encounters and end up dead. The media displays death through the context of their preset narrative: "white police officer, unarmed black man, with video footage." They dig through the 50 million police encounters per year searching for one to rile up their base. Every action of the police officer is scrutinized and minor mistakes fuel outrage and protest. Chants of racism fill the streets without much investigation into the facts.

The media reduces it to a split-second decision bias—but can you assign racism to something that happened so quickly? One second someone is reaching for a gun trying to kill you, the next they are running away. You have so much adrenaline pumping—you pull the trigger. Should you go to jail for the rest of your life for a position we put you in?

A vast majority of these recent problems stem from an uncooperative criminal element that does not desire a peaceful interaction. Words like "freeze" or "show me your hands" lose all meaning to criminals suffering from Antisocial Personality Disorder (ASPD). What is ASPD? It is a fancy way of saying, "I do what I want." Now we have a psychological medical leftist philosophical term treating the criminal as a victim of ASPD. Did they lack free will? Did they succumb to an environmental bacterium? Perhaps they chose to defy our laws for personal gain? Should it really matter? Should we try to rationalize irrational behavior?

Lost in all the noise are the actual victims. If one has ASPD, giving them a diagnosis does not prevent their behavior. Once we start excusing behavior based on a "mental illness" we fail to live in a civilized society. Most criminals have some type of mental issue or bad childhood, but they must still pay for their choices. If we fail to hold people accountable, then crime will grow. They are not worthy of our mercy, or our diagnoses.

Most police try to de-escalate these out of control situations. Few cops want to be in those deadly force encounters, where they may die or make a mistake and lose their freedom. Even if their actions are justified, there are months of paperwork and legal counseling. Being a police officer is a difficult job and takes a special character. Over 99.9% of police encounters are peaceful.

However, the media has done their best to unearth a once true narrative of systemic racism by white police officers. The left feeds off emotion and requires a political charge to rally its base against Republicans. During the murder of George Floyd, we witnessed this horrible rare storm of a story that fit the media narrative perfectly. Our nation was unanimous in its condemnation of the officer's actions. However, the mob could not be satisfied. Many cities burned and people died due to the ensuing riots and chaos.

This event was an anomaly, a rare instance of unthinkable human action leading to a tragic death. It does not require a law to fix or a new government to replace the old. Sometimes in life, we have the unthinkable, we can only react and try to prevent it. Were the officers racist? Without evidence, we cannot know.

This was an abuse of power. An officer who felt like he was above the law and put his knee on another human being's neck for 7 minutes and 46 seconds, ignoring all the pleas for common decency from the crowd and the victim. Did it kill him? Probably, but George Floyd also had hypertensive heart disease, the virus, and a lethal dose of fentanyl in his system. He was acting erratic and his exact cause of death needs to play out in a courtroom, not on a cable news channel.

That is not to justify the actions of the officers; they were wrong and reacted poorly. George Floyd was having some kind of panic attack and what should have been done differently needs to be discussed. The situation was turbulent from the beginning, Floyd was perhaps falsely accused of using counterfeit money and refused to get in the back of a squad car. What made this story so hard to swallow was that he did not seem like a hardened criminal but a troubled man in a state of fear and panic.

Something more egregious happened in Dallas during August of 2016 to a man named Tony Timpa. However, it did not fit the narrative because he was white so the mainstream media ignored it. Despite significant video evidence of a man pleading for his life with an officer's knee in his back, no charges were filed. The officers joked as the paramedic said this man is not breathing. They were back on the force after a short spineless investigation. It was an opportunity for the Black Lives Matter movement to step in and show they are truly about police reform for all people. Similar stores have happened to members of the Hispanic community but of no coverage. All of these events are great tragedies and proof that we must keep the police in check.

However, we do not live in a world of blue and black. Where the officer represents some blue tribe and therefore retaliation must take place on a different officer in a different city. This is a very dangerous game that leads to civil disobedience, innocent death, and anarchy. Good police are important for people of all colors.

This dangerous propaganda has extreme consequences. People get so bent by this narrative they walk up to police and open fire. Notably, in Compton, CA without warning a suspect opened fire on two officers. Now a 31 year old mother is fighting for her life in critical condition because some villain hates her job. To add insult to injury, BLM protesters showed up blocking the St. Francis Medical Center Emergency Entrance chanting, "we hope they die, " and "f*** the police." Who can defend this type of evil?

We need to emotionally divest ourselves from people that do not follow basic lawful commands. Generally speaking, the sidewalk is not a courtroom people need to respectfully obey the police, and wait for their day in court. We have yet to see a viral video where the commands of the officer were followed. If a person is in compliance and the officer shoots them then it is pure murder and he should rot in jail. But when people start arguing with officers, it gets murky and never seems to end well for anybody.

Jacob Blake was another recent case in Kenosha, Wisconsin. Where a white police officer shot a black man in the back 7 times with video footage. The headline spawned outrage but the nuanced facts had to be downplayed. This case was so close to being a perfect story netting political capital for the Democrats. So the media decided to amplify the race card and ignore certain details. After doing extensive research it is very difficult to find all the facts of this case. Our media is hopelessly bent.

One specific detail ignored was the second cell phone, camera angle which showed the initial confrontation with police. From the first cell phone it seems that an innocent man was just trying to get into his car when he was shot. It does not show the beginning of the confrontation. The second cell phone video shows Blake wrestling with officers and resisting arrest before going around the car.

Jacob Blake had active warrants out for his arrest (third-degree sexual assault, trespassing, and disorderly conduct in connection with domestic abuse) when his ex-girlfriend called police claiming Blake was trying to steal her key's and vehicle. Officers arrived and presumably tried to arrest Jacob. He resisted fighting with the officers and apparently putting one of them in a headlock. They tried to taser him twice to no avail.

According to the officers, they first saw a knife on the passenger side of the vehicle. Blake then walked around the driver's side of his car, opened his door, and reached inside. The officer yelled "Drop the Knife! Drop the Knife!" and he was shot. A knife was found on the floorboard of his vehicle, therefore it appears Blake was armed with a deadly weapon.

The key question in any of this is what should the police officers have done differently? They arrive and a man has warrants, they need to arrest him, and he resists. They try to force him into cuffs, he fights them off and gets away. He is allegedly armed at some point with a knife. Should they have let him drive away with children in the back? What would a "liberal" officer have done in this situation? Let him reach in his car hoping he would pull out a bouquet of flowers?

We could go back and forth all day about what the officers could have done differently, but the person that needed to change the most was the suspect. When the police come to make an arrest we need to cooperate. As Americans, we must not support a man who has actively defied our laws especially resisting arrest and alleged domestic abuse.

The Democrats were eager to swoop in and cash in some political points. After visiting with Blake, Kamala Harris said she was "proud" of a man who allegedly sexually assaulted his ex in front of their child. Isn't she supposed to be a supporter of the #metoo movement? Someone that stood up to Brett Kavanah and Joe Biden or was that just because it was in her political interest. The hypocrisy is sickening.

Graphic details of the assault from his ex-girlfriend:

*His ex-girlfriend stated that at about 6AM she was woken up by the father of her children, Jacob Blake, standing over her saying, "I want my s***." His ex-girlfriend lay there, on her back, the defendant, suddenly and without warning, reached his hand between her legs, penetrated her *** with a finger, pull it out and sniffed it, and said, "Smells like you've been with other men."*

Officer Raiche reported his ex-girlfriend had a very difficult time telling him this and cried as she told how the defendant assaulted her and then the defendant immediately left the bedroom. His ex-girlfriend stated the defendant penetrating her digitally caused her pain and humiliation and was done without her consent. Then he stole her vehicle and fled.

She had a restraining order against Jacob Blake and he was forbidden from returning to her house, that is why she called the police. Apparently to stop him from terrorizing her. He was not there to break up a fight as his lawyer claimed, he was apparently there to torture and sexually assault his victim.

Joe Biden's campaign said he would not visit Kenosha because he did not want to upset the "peaceful nature" of the protest. Then he visited Kenosha because it turned out to be in his political interest. Probably because Trump went and Biden was losing ground by staying home.

Biden met with the father Jacob Blake Sr to show he stood against racism. Biden treated him like he was some kind of civil rights icon. Quite the opposite, the man posted bigoted things about Jews, white people, and black Republicans. Using slurs such as "Cracker Jew" on social media. This man needs no elevation. He is a modern-day racist wanting to hold mock trials for officers from a podium in front of an angry mob.

In the wake of Jacob Blake's shooting, Kenosha felt the full force of the leftward mob. Things were looted and burnt, a 71-year-old man was knocked out and mocked. Citizens banded together and tried to protect local businesses from being burned. Small armed militias formed to stop the anarchy because the police were ordered to stand down by the liberal political class.

After lifeguarding all day and removing graffiti from buildings, Kyle Rittenhouse was asked to help protect a small business. According to his lawyer, he was given a firearm to go with his med-kit and when the criminal mob came and started a dumpster fire, one of Kyle's group dared to put it out. This turned an already tense scene into an attempted lynching.

Kyle can be seen running around with a fire extinguisher, for his alleged crimes of "anti-arson" Kyle was chased down by the angry mob. A convicted white felon who was fond of using the n-word earlier that night, threw a white bag and yelled threats as he ran behind Kyle in hot pursuit. Another rioter pulled out a gun and shot it in the air. When the white felon caught up to Kyle, Kyle turned around and defended himself. This was a textbook case of self-defense in my opinion.

After Kyle ran toward the police line to turn himself in, the angry mob began to chase him down yelling that he had just shot someone. After catching up to him they knocked him to the ground and tried to pile-on, but he had other ideas and it did not end well for the angry mob.

The biased DA's office launched a multitude of criminal complaints against Kyle, but their filing looks like it was prepared by Kyle's defense attorney. The probable cause statement shows Kyle on the ground in a vulnerable position when one "victim" lunges at him with a skateboard and hits Kyle. Presumably to try and knock him unconscious, take his weapon, and beat him to death in the street.

Immediate mob justice? That is not how we do things in America. These charges are so obviously politically motivated. Wisconsin has a very strong self-defense statute. The media wanted this narrative to fit their idea so badly: white racist murdering peaceful BLM protesters. They wanted it to be like a school shooter going around indiscriminately killing but it clearly is not. So far it seems like self-defense but we shall see how it all plays out.

The left views "hate crime" as something different. It is an irredeemable crime, for which maximum sentencing must be imposed. The truth is all crimes are hate crimes, as we are all equal in the eyes of the law. Using special divisions and distinction for things that cause more emotional disturbance to certain groups of people is not just. We must attack all criminals with equal force if we are to have true justice.

Speaking from personal experience, I was a victim of an armed bank robbery. I felt the true meaning of ASPD. My life was worth nothing more than that of a roach to an exterminator. If he could have gained a dime more by shooting me in the head, he would have. There is no movie or video clip that could accurately transfer the stream of hopeless decay and anger I felt. Do I blame a system rigged against a man who from birth was forced into a life of crime? No, I blame someone who squandered
his educational opportunities and made selfish choices leading to detrimental outcomes. Until we put the blame squarely on the shoulders of those who make terrible choices, we will never reduce the problem.

The community outrage stems from the differential treatment of young black men. The thought is that when a white police officer approaches their car, his hand is closer to his gun. His mind is ready to react in a split second. Is this true? Is it justified?

We cannot know if it's true but in the eyes of the law, we should all be treated equally. No one group should be given preferential or differential treatment over another. Therefore, our law enforcement officers should approach everyone with the same posture. We would program our robot police this way, but for now we must live with our imperfect human beings taught by real-world statistical biases. How many white women that live in the affluent suburbs have pulled a gun and fired on cops?

The officers use stereotypes to reduce anxiety. Our brains work by simplifying threats so that we can focus on the real danger. We are hard-wired for this type of survival—it is in our DNA. On average, men kill significantly more than women—approximately 70-90% of all murders are committed by men. We need to confront it and try to fix it. Shooting it down as sexist does not help solve the problem.

The statistical truth is that black men comprise approximately 6% of the population, yet they account for over 50% of the murders and 30-40% of police homicides. In 2019 out of all the police interactions only 9 unarmed black men were killed by police. This hardly seems like genocide or systemic racism. Especially considering 20 unarmed white men were killed by police in that same year. While white people may outnumber black people, black people tend to commit more violent crimes. Being caught in the act of violent crime increases the chance of a tense police standoff and therefore a potential shooting. Based on those adjusted numbers there is no statistical significance between police killing black or white people.

One would not garner that interpretation listening to what Sandra L. Shullman, Ph.D, and president of the American Psychological Association had to say after George Floyd's death. "The deaths of innocent black people targeted specifically because of their race — often by police officers — are both deeply shocking and shockingly routine." She added, "If you're black in America — and especially if you are a black male - it's not safe to go birding in Central Park, to meet friends at a Philadelphia Starbucks, to pick up trash in front of your own home in Colorado or to go shopping almost anywhere." Finally, she said, "We are living in a racism pandemic, which is taking a heavy psychological toll on our African American citizens." .

The inner-city community knows first-hand how dangerous the streets can be. These numbers need to be dealt with by Democratic leaders. Not ignored and downplayed as racist. That does not help anything. We must be brave and push for solutions. Do people that openly chant "F the police" helping anything? Is it due to a culture that does not respect law and order? Why are so many families damaged or destroyed? What role does the larger community play? Entirely too many children grow up without a father in the home. How does this affect them? What can we do to help?

Growing up with a father figure is important. People that say, "I cannot do that my dad would kill me!" are much better off than those that lack any real supervision. Respect for authority is crucial—a father in the home, a strong mother, the military, community leaders, teachers, church pastors, or coaches can all provide this. It is an absolute must. If you have free time, join a big-brother program and give the youth the respect and discipline they need to live a clean life.

The direction is also important to all youth of any color. They need to realize that helping humanity is our greatest purpose. It is a difficult task because many times the things we think help, hurt. The best thing to do is guide them in the right direction and give them purpose.

We must break down the hatred that exists. No more pushing the slavery narrative on our youth, or making them think the racist system is out to get them. How can you strive for success when you believe the system is broken? When these emotions subside, we can transcend.

The police are not the enemy—the larger community created them to protect freedom. The media pollutes our minds with half-truths. They act as political opportunists increasing their power base. This creates dangerous transference, which makes our communities less safe.

In every bunch, there are a few bad apples, and police are no different. The best way to root them out is with sunlight such as body cams, dash cams, and internal affairs. Keeping an eye on police is a worthwhile endeavor, as there are many important freedoms at stake, but we must do this with respect because most cops are good cops
Our default should not be with the argumentative, uncooperative criminals. We must unite behind our men and women in blue unless factual circumstance indicates otherwise. Failing to do this will weaken our police forces and reduce the opportunities for the underprivileged youth to grow up in crime-free neighborhoods.

Cops are working-class people that overwhelmingly vote Republican. Thus, they are expendable to the elitist and problematic for criminal anarchists. These two forces have united to defund the police. From the top down they are being hamstrung by those who control Democratic mayors. From the bottom up they are being destroyed by a lawless criminal element bent on anarchy. In the middle are the Democrats who will do anything for power. Even if it means letting cities burn and looters riot. If they think it is a winning platform then they will watch it happen. There is no moral code in them other than victory. They chase it around like a cat following a light. Trump has successfully blamed the politicians in Democrat-run Cities for the chaos and violence.

There has been a shift due to Trump's successfully labeling them "Democrat Run Cities." Now the mayors and governors fecklessly try to fight problems in their cities. Not because they care about lives and property but because it is showing up in the poll numbers. Police need our support and we need police to function properly. In a brilliant move, Trump deputized Oregon State Police officers; in an attempt to bypass the corrupt DA's and prosecute some of the Communist criminals.

Is it their fault? They let rioters out the next day and drop charges for no reason. Failing to hold criminals accountable will only create more crime. The leftist who shot Aaron Danielson in Portland should have been in jail for weapons charges. Perhaps because he has the "right" political persuasion the charges were dropped without comment. Even in the case of murder, Democrats will support Democrats.

The media twisted and ignored the story. Trying to downplay it as if the Trump supporters driving around Portland were somehow responsible for the agitations of a homicidal mob. Showing support for the American president in an American city is unacceptable? The BLM/Antifa movement rejoiced in his execution, the media ignores their rally in which they cheer on his death. They are grotesquely applauding a murder. The left refuses to hold its members accountable because to them it is not about morals or facts, it is about allegiance and power. The web of liberalism is all that matters and one is either inside and protected or outside and hated.

Their mayors handicap the police to appease the angry mob. They take away basic tools such as tear gas, pepper spray, and rubber bullets. These things are designed to fight off large hordes of rioters without using deadly force. The left vilifies hard-working police and makes them hate their job. This will only make police forces weaker.

The left-wing has created a frenzy over an isolated incident of police brutality to galvanize an immature mob. Now they feel justified in blaming the people they hurl rocks at for angering them enough to windup. The left ignores a basic principle; people are less likely to sympathize with a movement that annoys them. Burning down a city does not endear its residents to a cause. It just alienates people and makes radicals look like jerks.

What is more, Liberals need to have a cohesive message and a precise piece of legislation to advocate for. Having a protest without these basic things is ignorant. Millions marched for black lives but did not properly articulate their message. What exactly do they want? To end all bad police shootings? This is like trying to end all crime. It is a great idea on the surface but nearly impossible to implement. Humans are prone to error and police are humans.

The left is an immature mob that must be sat down and explained to with patience and strength. They will not respect weakness only grow more irrational from it. We must take the time to elect representatives that will explain to them how all these crazy ideas sound great on paper (x) but when you try to implement them the result is catastrophic (y). Do police free zones sound like utopia? Only to a leftist and only until it devolves into a lawless slum with power predators preying on the weak.

Professors pump our young impressionable youth with socialist propaganda. They continually pass on their elitist contagion which divides our great nation. Perhaps, it is brought about by a sense of mental superiority, a type of half-witted arrogance that is responsible for some of the worst atrocities in human history.

Like many things in politics and life, this is a balancing act, and we can make two legitimate arguments. The justice system has to take freedom from criminals, yet maintain it for law-abiding citizens. It is imperative that we carefully examine each situation and make the best decisions; otherwise, it tears away at the fabric of our country. We cannot allow anyone to be bullied by the police, and we cannot persecute police put in dangerous situations with uncooperative criminals.

Thinking about this emotional landscape is individualistic. Opinions are slow to change even when presented with facts. Facts injure the delicate psyche built up around false beliefs. Therefore, facts must be stifled and the left hunts down opposition to destroy it, if not, they will cause emotional harm. This is a dangerous mentality, especially in an open and free society. People need to be educated enough to understand the context, as we should never advocate censorship.

Communism

We have all heard of the "spread of communism" and the "red scare" but communism is an idea that no civilization has ever truly implemented. This is proof that it is impractical on a large scale. Most of the governments that have been called communists, such as the Soviet Union, China, Cuba, North Korea, were/are actually more socialist. However, for the sake of argument, we will consider them communist.

At its most ideological level, communism is an attempt at creating a perfect society—removing the currency and class systems, and living in harmony with one and other. In a true communist society, there are no rich and no poor, all outcomes are equal. In communism, everyone works for the nation-state, and everyone benefits from it.

If one were to journey on a small spacecraft with 10-20 people, one would likely live in a state of communism. It would work well in this situation, as everyone would complete a job, and everyone would get a bunk and an equal ration. There would be no need for currency or competition. The reason it works so well here is that there is nothing natural about this scenario. The captain has been pre-selected to be judicious and fair, the flight crew is confident and capable, and the bad apples never made it on board. Also, everyone is immediately accountable to the whole.

On a larger scale, this attempt at a perfect hive-like society has many unintended consequences. Firstly, a rising tsar would have control of the private sector as well as the government—in essence, making him the king of everything. This type of power inevitably corrupts, and a despotic regime will ultimately ensue.

The second problem is motivation—which is dependent on patriotism. As the people's perception of their government changes then so do their productivity levels. People can be easily disaffected, which causes instability and mass poverty. In many casesm people feel stuck, as it is impossible to advance, which creates hopelessness. Would we be happy if we could never get a raise or promotion? It also requires sharp and sometimes violent reprimands of disloyal freeloaders.

Imagine if all the people who despised Donald Trump and/or Barack Obama had to go to work for the good of the Trump/Obama Regime. How hard would they work? Would they strike? Moreover, if they did would the governments have to put down the strike with force? Would the people starve if the government did nothing? Therefore, the unnatural state of communism leads to totalitarianism. Productivity is not linked to self-interest; instead, it is linked to patriotism, which changes based on feelings.

The unforgivable third problem is that it is inherently anti-freedom. This necessity for allegiance and good feelings prompts the need for brainwashing. The state controls everything—therefore belief in the state must be absolute, thus propaganda. The media is put on a very tight leash. Freedom of speech is not possible in a communist society. Freedom of religion, the right to own property, and fair elections are watered down by those in power.

Additionally, there is no balancing party in a communist society. As much as Democrats and Republicans might dislike each other, our system works because of that animosity. In a communist society, the leaders squelch opposition. They do this because the voice of freedom is overwhelmingly powerful. If it is not extinguished, it will spread like a wildfire burning down the entire regime. Therefore, they must create "Red Curtains" and "Propaganda Posters."

Communism is like slavery for an entire society. Everyone gets work, room & board, and a severe lack of choices. People are not free to pursue their dreams; they are wards of the state. The powerful pick the path and crack the whip should anyone step out of the two-mile bread line. Competition dies because the focus is on keeping the masses productive—instead of the self-interested individuals competing to lift the entire society organically. People tend to search for the easiest way out. Therefore, communist leaders build a system of not letting them. Forcing humans to interact and be productive in this way is pure oppression and freedom becomes a bad word.

How much freedom one has depends on how communistic the society is. Many modern communist countries have moved away from the Gulags and censorship. As people become less isolated, it is more difficult to oppress them. Modern inventions like the smartphone with its apps help us to connect and avoid curtains.

Socialism

Socialism in its many forms is a hybrid of communism and capitalism. Every major government is socialist. However, we will define it by the European/Canadian version. Socialist governments have some free enterprise mixed with a limit on the suffering of the poor, providing them with education, food, and healthcare. This is a soft society full of safety nets and rubber padding. It is the ultimate participation trophy club full of equal outcomes and reduced ingenuity.

In socialism, the government owns some means of production and provides some free services, such as healthcare, education, and welfare. The negative side effects are far less dramatic than communism. The Democratic leaders allow rival ideas and parties; however, individual liberty is not typically celebrated.

Society considers the whole more important than the individual—therefore they will penalize successful people for the greater good. The people in socialism work for the government instead of the government working for the people. Taxes are inevitably high and society does not celebrate achievement unless attained by a victim class. Freedoms, such as speech, are not welcomed if they damage or hinder members of the society. Many socialist countries have strict limits on "hate speech" and even put people in jail for it.

Ideally, if one were to run society in a university lab experiment, they might favor this type of government. In theory, the model of it should work well, but in reality, we find it to have a weaker output. It limits freedoms and the individual opportunity for success. It is not a natural form of governance, but an unnatural attempt at perfect outcomes. It requires the hubris to think we can end suffering; however, when mixed with sufficient capitalism, it can function effectively.

Capitalism

Then we have capitalism, a system based on individual freedom. America has the closest form of capitalism, the idea that we own ourselves and all our means of production. Ultimately, we will sink or swim based on that skill set. If we sink, we will be eating dirt and if we swim, we will own the dirt.

Capitalism is the most Darwinian of the governmental systems, in that the strong CEO survives, and the weak homeless starve. This is the natural order because a person who works hard, goes to school for years, and provides the society with what it needs, should be rewarded. A person who drops out of school because they thought it was dumb should not be allowed to leech off the success of another. Socialism blows out the flame of the American Dream, while capitalism ignites incentive.

In some ways, capitalism can seem callous and cold, but so is watching a lion eat a gazelle. In nature, the strength of the hunter determines the size of the feast. This is the order of the natural world, and it is better than living in a state full of taxes - a government that steals half our meat at the edge of the forest, and then decides who eats. Sometimes they give it to a capable person who has not done a day of work in their life. It is not the American way and it is not freedom. Those who do not work do not deserve, and those who cannot work should rely on charity.

Would it be better if the person leaving the woods with meat stopped by the genuinely needy person's home and offered them some meat? This is far better than forcing it from their hand—the very hand that hunted it down. This is a sustainable society—one where relationships matter and the love we have for each other is not forced.

Survival is a powerful incentive and to deprive some of this motivational force is to weaken them. There are no safety nets in the wild and we are only creating a weaker generation by catering to this. Take your meat home with you and let them sink or swim. Unlike a communist society, we are not overly dependent on each other.

People who realize this are the most successful business people in the world, and their success lifts the people around them. They employ thousands and pay them millions. These lions are the reason America is the most powerful country in the world.

We have voluntarily come together to share in a society, and if we deprive people of the greatest incentive of all, that of the cold hard ground when they fail, then we are not living in a sustainable world.

The fundamental question to answer is, "which system makes us stronger?" Many of us are charitable individuals who do not mind lending a helping hand; the problem is the same as feeding stray dogs. Once we feed them then there are twenty more at the door; we create a codependent relationship. This weakens our society in an attempt to prevent suffering.

The bottom line is that capitalism stresses competition and profit; this competition drives the individual beyond their ordinary limitations, and the profit rewards them. Capitalism is based on free enterprise—people have the right and freedom to own land and businesses. Socialism and communism call for group cooperation. They represent a beehive society with everyone producing the honey to pay for the social services.

The biggest flaw in capitalism is that capital will tend to coalesce around the top. The government needs to manage this—acting as a referee. In an unregulated market, the powerful will use their wealth to stifle competition and opportunity will die. This is especially apparent with modern technology; a group connected with Silicon Valley will have a massive advantage over any new competition. The antitrust laws are necessary because without freedom of opportunity the American Dream cannot live.

Why?

Upon reading all these facts we are only left with one question: Why would anyone support the left? The reason is simple greed. People's self-interest overrules their moral objections. This type of thought will always seek to contaminate our political discourse. It is not rare; in fact, America is the exception. Throughout human history, we have been ruled by tyrants. The Elites infiltrate by promising the underclass a better life with less evil white Karens in exchange for votes and a blank check on corruption. The young impressionable liberals get sold on the moral high-ground of being anti-racist. They want so desperately to fit in they will mix the Kool-Aid themselves, and drink the amalgamation of contradictions.

They could never read this book or go through my text line by line and refute it because truth does not matter. Whether Joe Biden is a racist, corrupt Washington political insider does not matter to them, all that matters is that he is in their tent and everything Trump is evil. Because they only know teams.

Balance Theory

Right now the left controls our media, House of Representatives, educational institutions, and entertainment industry. The right controls talk radio, the Supreme Court, the Senate, and the presidency. To give the presidency or Senate to the left would cause irreparable harm to the balance of power. Especially considering how out of control and united the left is. They will use the full weight of the federal government to go after political rivals like Mike Flynn and Carter Paige. They fantasize about bringing Trump's children up on charges. No stone will be left unturned in their vile vengeance tour.

They will use the justice department to destroy the NRA and the IRS to tax conservative groups. They will use the FCC to regulate Fox News and the EPA to destroy businesses. They will use the FBI and CIA to destroy anyone not in agreement. Our nation will be greatly set back by taxes and out of control welfare spending. China will leap ahead of us as the lone global superpower.

After a Democratic process, Donald John Trump is our best option. He is willing to carry out the will of the people. His approach may not be suitable for some, but his results will be good for all. Respect it and if the media wants to wage a "war of words" then do it against the American people, we elected Trump and we will do it again.

10 Strikes Against Biden

X   Health Concerns

Considering the stress of the White House and Biden's age in office 78-82, it would be cruel to push him into the presidency. Aneurysms, risk of stroke, and cognitive decline could all lead to an awkward 25th amendment battle. Not to mention handing off the nuclear football to someone suffering from obvious mental decline.

X   His Number Two

He chose a radical in Kamala Harris and proved how much control the far-left has over him. Her divisive nature would wreck our hope for unity. She is a bitter partisan unwilling to reach across the aisle. Instead she threatens to rule by executive action.

X   The Leftist Agenda is Destructive

Thirty years ago it was a slur to call someone a socialist now it is a badge of honor. Over time we forget the negative consequences of socialism. His platform has been hijacked by the radical-left with their extreme agenda.

X   He is Part of the Political Establishment

Joe Biden is the swamp. He has been in Washington for 44 years and has not really accomplished anything except make himself rich to the tune of $16 million.

X   He is Corrupt

He peddled political influence through his son Hunter Biden selling-out our country.

X   He Will Put China First

Joe Biden said a rising China is a good thing for America. The left refuses to stand against China. Liberals claim to be against oppression and slavery but refuse to speak out against an oppressive regime. Proving they are not a party of bedrock principals. If the polls forced Biden to change on China he would. Now, he finally wants to get tough on China, a welcomed flip-flop.

X   He is an Excessive Flip-Flopper

Sometimes politicians change positions but Joe Biden is beyond the pale. There are too many to list: Abortion, Crime, Segregation, guns, China, visiting Kenosha, NAFTA, Iraq War, being a progressive.. He has pulled the rare flip-flop-flip on the Hyde Amendment.

X   He is not Transparent

He rarely communicates directly with the American people. His speeches and interviews with pre-approved questions are scripted and read off Teleprompters.

X   He Lies

He imagines things that give him a political advantage are true; such as finishing at the top of his law class, being a civil rights icon, saying he was not going to cut social security. He promises not to raise taxes but is somehow going to collaborate with Sanders & Aoc. He lies to have it both ways.

X   He is a Racist

He befriended racist, made racist comments, and wrote racist legislation.